A PURPOSEFUL
PATH

A PURPOSEFUL PATH

HOW FAR CAN YOU GO WITH $30, A BUS TICKET, AND A DREAM?

CASEY BEAUMIER, SJ

LOYOLA PRESS.
A JESUIT MINISTRY
Chicago

LOYOLA PRESS.
A JESUIT MINISTRY

3441 N. Ashland Avenue
Chicago, Illinois 60657
(800) 621-1008
www.loyolapress.com

Imprimi potest: Very Rev. Thomas A. Lawler, SJ, provincial

Scripture excerpts are taken from the *New American Bible with Revised New Testament and Psalms*, Copyright 1991, 1986, 1970 by the Confraternity of Christian Doctrine, Washington, DC. Used with permission. All rights reserved. No part of the *New American Bible* may be reproduced in any form without permission in writing from the copyright owner.

Cover art credit: Top image, Giakita/iStock/Thinkstock, bottom image, Meredith Adelaide/Stocksy.

ISBN-13: 978-0-8294-4250-2
ISBN-10: 0-8294-4250-2
Library of Congress Control Number: 2014958518

Printed in the United States of America.

15 16 17 18 19 20 Versa 10 9 8 7 6 5 4 3 2 1

What are you looking at me for? . . .
I just come to tell you, it's Easter Day.
—Maya Angelou, *I Know Why the Caged Bird Sings*

Goodness always tends to spread.
Every authentic experience of truth and goodness seeks
by its very nature to grow within us,
and any person who has experienced a
profound liberation
becomes more sensitive to the needs of others.
As it expands, goodness takes root and develops.
If we wish to lead a dignified and fulfilling life,
we have to reach out to others and seek their good.
—Pope Francis, *Evangelii Gaudium*

Contents

1

Foundations

From the very first paragraph I know that I like her.

I pause after the opening few pages and put the book down on my desk. I am connecting with her. I don't quite understand why—but I want to.

Maya Angelou begins her autobiography with a flashback to an Easter morning in her childhood. She's standing in front of the whole church congregation, and she's nervous.

"What you looking at me for?"

It's supposed to be a beautiful moment. She's supposed to make an Easter recitation. But she stumbles.

Her self-consciousness overwhelms her. She freezes. She just can't get the words out. The other kids are laughing. Escape is her only option. She bursts out of the church, peeing and crying.

Then I have a flashback.

I am a child. I'm overweight and self-conscious. I try to hide in the classroom.

"What you looking at me for . . .?"

I, too, want to run out. My sour release is nervous sweat. I sweat so profusely that every day I sneak into the restroom during each passing period and grab a stack of paper towels to stuff discreetly under my armpits in my feeble attempt to hide it from the kids.

I know that they will laugh.

I'm supposed to be happy. I pass the hours with my arms pinched close to my sides to keep the soggy paper in place. As I journey through those young days, everything about me is tight. I'm just trying to hold it together so that nobody sees me sweat.

I blink the tears from my eyes, and then suddenly I'm brought back from the past as I return to being a freshman in my college dorm room. I'm so different from when I was a child. I'm no longer fat. I am more outgoing. I have grown up, and I am in college. It's supposed to be fun.

But if I am quite honest with myself, I know that something has just happened because of the power of words.

I pick up the book again. The pages expose to my heart what I don't quite want to see. I am still so self-conscious. I am very afraid of the journey.

But in this moment I know that I am not alone. I just made a friend: Maya Angelou. Here she is with me in my dorm room. She is in the words on the paper in my hands. I'm staring at the pages until I see her in the words. I lean in to gaze deeper until the words open my ears and I can actually hear her. Her words speak to me at the very beginning.

What are you looking at me for? . . .
I just come to tell you it's Easter Day.

From that moment, college became a prolonged Easter Day—an increasingly lively living where my heart and mind overflowed with new life. I met marvelous friends. I loved journalism. I experienced the city as exhilarating. All this took place at a Jesuit school: Marquette University in Milwaukee, Wisconsin.

I admit that when I first began my studies, I didn't really know what Jesuits were or what it meant for Marquette to be a Jesuit university. That changed abruptly when I became an RA, a resident advisor, for freshmen.

A Jesuit priest lived in each dorm at Marquette, and I became close to our Jesuit chaplain, Father William Leahy. Many students sought him out for counsel. He was easy to talk with.

Father Leahy became a mentor for me. Before I entered senior year, I paused to consider the direction of my life. I planned on becoming a journalist. Yet when I reflected on how I spent most of my time and what brought delight to my heart, my plans changed.

When senior year began, I decided that I wanted to become a Jesuit.

I applied and entered the Jesuits right out of college. When a person enters the Jesuits, he is a novice—a beginner. Each novice undergoes several experiments, which help both him and the leadership within the Jesuits test the solidity of his vocation and whether he should continue to move forward in the lengthy Jesuit formation process. All the experiments of the novitiate are based on the religious conversion experienced by the founder of the Jesuits, Saint Ignatius of Loyola.

The first experiment that a Jesuit novice undergoes is to make a thirty-day silent retreat of intense prayer called *The Spiritual Exercises*. Written by Saint Ignatius, the *Exercises* are regarded today as a spiritual classic. At the very beginning of *The Spiritual Exercises* Ignatius describes what he experiences and names as the First Principle and Foundation. It is just as it sounds, that solid ground upon which every other thing in this life is to be sturdily constructed. It is that foundation to which Jesus Christ speaks in chapter 7 of Matthew's Gospel, in the parable about the ground upon which to build one's house:

> Everyone who listens to these words of mine and acts on them
> will be like a wise man who built his house on rock. The rain fell,
> the floods came, and the winds blew and buffeted the house. But
> it did not collapse; it had been set solidly on rock.

Ignatius says this about the foundational purpose of life: human beings are created to praise, reverence, and serve God, and by means of doing this they shall save their souls. To have this life purpose implies a deep and loving relationship between God the Father and every human being. If I am to praise, reverence, and serve God, then I am to love the Lord with all my heart, soul, mind, strength—my entire being. Love between God and persons propels and deepens this way of living on such a firm and stable foundation.

I have come to realize that if loving God in this absolute fullness of my being is the foundation of life—the reason I was created—then my life will thrive upon this love.

Love continually flows back and forth between God and me because that is the nature of love—it is reciprocal. Such love begins with God, and in freedom I am invited to accept this love to make my corresponding loving response. Each day I desire to know with ever-increasing joy that I am loved unconditionally. My response to this deepening interior knowledge of the heart is to love God in return through my praise, reverence, and service.

Nobody can force this grace upon another person—such divine love must be experienced directly and in total freedom by the person if it is to be transformative. It is neither possible nor proper for me to try to convince you of this truth, because it is an article of Christian faith; there can be no coercion when it comes to receptivity of God's love. That's why Christians believe that if this unconditional love is received freely, it will be experienced as absolutely irresistible and completely transformative. In response, a person will be filled with the desire to offer, in return, a profound love for God.

Much can happen during this retreat experiment of thirty days of contemplative silence. One of the spiritual gifts I received was simple yet profound. I came to understand the beating of the human heart as direct communication from God of his approval of and desire for my very existence. I believe that the heartbeat can be recognized as a gentle and constant reminder that the Father has willed every human being into existence simply because of his profound and unconditional love for humanity, especially and specifically for every single person.

It isn't easy to articulate this reality. The heart—the soul—is the center, the core of a human being and the place where this identity rests. Christians believe that every single person is a beloved child of the Father and therefore, a companion; a friend of Christ Jesus, and therefore, a temple of the Holy Spirit.

Every other thing a human being experiences in the course of a lifetime is secondary to this core identity. Every experience, every relationship, every desire we have occurs simply to reinforce this primary core identity. That means that everything in human life is a gift given to remind humans of who they *really* are as beloved daughters and sons of God. Everything that *is* exists solely to strengthen the core.

This marvelous truth contains within it also the source of every human pain: to perceive what is meant to be secondary in life as something primary. This is what is meant by *disorder*: mistakenly believing that a secondary gift in life is actually one's primary identity. But every secondary gift, whatever it is, has been given to build up the core of who you are as a beloved child of God. Everything secondary exists to reveal more profoundly what is primary in human life.

Let's say a person loves to play football. In high school he eats, drinks, and sleeps football. He loves it so much that it practically consumes him. Well, sooner or later this person will no longer be able to play football, perhaps because of an injury or because of age. If he has made football the core of his being, then he is going to get hurt because his incorrect thinking will lead him to utter frustration. The truth is that he does not exist on this earth to be a football player. He wasn't born to play that game; he was born to be loved. His love for football is a secondary gift that has been given to help him know more profoundly that God loves him.

The constant temptation in the earthly life always is to make our secondary identities primary. Football player, earthly daughter, best friend, volleyball player, student, administrator, lawyer, teacher . . . all are gifts given to strengthen the core. All will pass away, because that is the way secondary gifts work. To be tempted to absolutize a secondary identity—claiming it as primary and therefore permanent—is something human beings do all the time, and it always results in pain. This is *the* human struggle of life.

So, part of the purpose in the earthly life is to live every day knowing who one really is as a beloved child of God, enjoying all the secondary gifts that life brings, while standing confidently on the firm foundation of life. Pedro Arrupe, a Spanish Jesuit who led the Society of Jesus in the 1960s and '70s received a beautiful prayer that articulates this dynamic of daily life:

> Nothing is more practical than finding God,
> than falling in Love in a quite absolute, final way.
> What you are in love with, what seizes your imagination,
> will affect everything.
> It will decide what will get you out of bed in the morning,
> what you will do with your evenings,
> how you will spend your weekends,
> what you read, whom you know,
> what breaks your heart,

and what amazes you with joy and gratitude.
Fall in Love, stay in love, and it will decide everything.

When you and I recognize from whom all good things come, something within us wants to be close to that generous source: God's love. Once a person taps into such love, everything has its rightful place in life. Human beings are then able, in the words of the Indian Jesuit Anthony de Mello, "to hold and not to cling, enjoy and not possess."

This understanding of the First Principle and Foundation has become the center of my daily prayer as a Jesuit, but not without struggle. There are many secondary identities that I have long fancied as essential to who I am. I've given into the temptation to cling to them, and I've had to learn repeatedly that doing so always leads to frustration.

In 1994, when I was making the Spiritual Exercises as a Jesuit novice in Denver, Colorado, this foundation was established in my heart and mind in a way that I could understand it at that time in my life, although my comprehension was clearly that of a beginner. I loved those days of silent prayer. Near the end of the thirty days the retreat culminates with a special and final consideration of unconditional divine love. The person making the Exercises is then sent out of silence back into the world to spend his or her life on others, fortified and fueled by this interior knowledge of the heart. The desire is to live in the world joyfully and generously, rooted in interior freedom while simultaneously finding God in the gift of all sorts of secondary identities. This concluding meditation is called the "Contemplation to Attain Divine Love" and with the introductory "Foundation," they make the bookends of those thirty days of silence.

On most afternoons during that month of spiritual exercises we novices often went to make some physical exercises at the YMCA in downtown Denver. Sometimes when I was returning from the gym to our Jesuit house on Eudora Street I would make a brief visit to a bookstore, Tattered Cover, to do some spiritual reading in a different venue. Near the end of the month I walked into the store and noticed a newly placed book display. Upon it were neatly arranged copies of a new release. A new title, *Wouldn't Take Nothing for My Journey Now*, caught my eye. The title seemed to speak to me of what I was learning about secondary identities. In life's journey, you can't take them with you. Then I saw the author: Maya Angelou. While I had continued to admire her during my college years, I hadn't kept up with her writing. When I opened up the book, the pages fell to an entry titled "The Power of the Word." Maybe that title captured my attention because I had been living in silence and was longing for spoken (written) words that would correspond to the words I had experienced during my days of silence.

One day the teacher, Frederick Wilkerson, asked me to read to him. I was 24, very erudite, very worldly. He asked that I read from Lessons in Truth, a section which ended with these words: "God loves me." I read the piece and closed the book, and the teacher said, "Read it again." I pointedly opened the book, and I sarcastically read, "God loves me." He said, "Again."

After about the seventh repetition I began to sense that there might be truth in the statement, that there was a possibility that God really did love me. Me, Maya Angelou. I suddenly began to cry at the grandness of it all. I knew that if God loved me, then I could do wonderful things. I could try great things, learn anything, achieve anything. For what could stand against me with God, since one person, any person with God, constitutes the majority?

That knowledge humbles me, melts my bones, closes my ears, and makes my teeth rock loosely in their gums. And it also liberates me. I am a big bird winging over high mountains, down into serene valleys. I am ripples of waves on silver seas. I am a spring leaf trembling in anticipation.

As I read, I experienced a sort of convergence of heaven and earth. It was not a coincidence that I would be led to such a passage at that time, for those words spoke precisely of what I was living as I prepared to finish thirty days of a retreat so deeply rooted in the power of the word: sacred Scripture. Angelou had written about her own reception of the unconditional love of God and what that love was capable of doing to facilitate the transformation of human life. She was able to articulate so much more clearly what was happening within me at that very moment. I sat down, took out my journal, and copied that little bit of text. Over the years my eyes have returned often to that page.

What occurred next convinced me that God's hand was at work, building upon this foundation of love. It placed my life on an entirely new trajectory.

2

Vision

The second experiment a Jesuit novice undergoes is what we call *Hospital.* The point of the experiment is to move from the graced, contemplative experience of the Spiritual Exercises into active service for humanity. In other words, to give oneself to the labor of building up God's kingdom on earth as it is in heaven. In this moment of leaving the silence of the retreat, a Jesuit feels his life propelled into service, fueled by divine love. So confident is he of the unconditional love of the Father that he desires to serve God in all things. He wants to give himself away to something greater than himself, which we Christians believe to be the kingdom of God. On the hospital experiment, a Jesuit serves the vulnerable population of humanity, usually the elderly, the sick, or the handicapped.

In the early 1990s, many of the American Jesuit novices were being sent for their hospital experiment to L'Arche communities. L'Arche is a Christian ministry of service to the mentally and physically handicapped. It began in France through the charism (spiritual gift) of a layman named Jean Vanier. Through him and the early members of the L'Arche movement, an entirely new Christian spirituality was born, mirrored in the biblical revelation of the inclusive ark of Noah, built as saving protection from a massive flood for the diversity of the Father's creation.

In L'Arche communities, this same desire to preserve the gift of creation is at work, with the handicapped living at the center of communal life because of the beauty and value of their lives. Many of the members of the community experienced lives of rejection prior to their entrance into the L'Arche community, but when they arrived, their lives were reclaimed for their interior value. They were protected and loved simply because of the goodness of their humanity.

The novice master sent my classmate Chris and me to the community in Toronto, Canada. This place was called Daybreak, and it consisted of a network of about twenty houses throughout metropolitan and suburban Toronto. Each house was composed of assistants and core members who lived in common, the vulnerability of humanity as the bond holding them together in love. We would serve as assistants in different houses.

Daybreak was an exciting place to be, as it was the home to the prolific author Henri Nouwen, a Catholic priest from the Netherlands who joined the L'Arche community in Canada to serve as a spiritual shepherd. I admired Nouwen's writings and recommend them still. He and many others gave us a warm welcome upon our arrival.

Within the Daybreak community I was assigned to work in the Corner House. This was a marvelous little home where four high school kids, three young women and one young man, lived as the core members of that community. I absolutely loved it—and I experienced the work as both very challenging and immensely satisfying. All four core members needed full bodily care—which included feeding, bathing, and dressing them. The assistants with whom I worked were incredibly generous and beautiful Christian people. I learned so much from them and through their encouragement. Because of their good example and mentoring, it was only a short time before I came to love this ministry. My classmate and I lived in an apartment nearby, and I remember both of us returning to it each night exhausted from work—we were completely spent at Daybreak—and satisfied.

It was easy for me to find God at L'Arche, which was the point of the experiment. It was easy, too, for me to pass time there, and I enjoyed having the opportunity to visit with a kind and wise Catholic nun named Sue Mosteller and the priest writer Henri Nouwen. He had completed a book on the topic of death and dying while we were there, and he gave each of us a copy of this book. He died only a few years after we met him. When I look back on that time in Toronto, I am grateful that part of the experience was living with someone who has helped so many others through the gift of writing.

During that time in Toronto we were given one day for rest each week. Often that day was scheduled differently from that of my classmate, so I usually spent it alone. We didn't have much money at all, and it was winter, so we spent most of the time taking the metro into the city and then walking around Toronto. I loved the city and found it easy to explore.

As I remember, it was during one of those days of walking around downtown Toronto that I began to examine more seriously a desire I had received for the next novice experiment we were to undertake following hospital. This third experiment is called *Pilgrimage*. The pilgrimage vision I was seeing while I was in Toronto had been planted in my heart toward the end of the thirty-day retreat. In fact, it had been planted at that bookstore in Denver.

While I wandered Toronto on those occasional break days, I found myself recalling how I had been led to that text at Tattered Cover at the end of the retreat. What I noticed in Toronto was that I was experiencing through the ministry at L'Arche the incarnation of what Maya Angelou had described through the power of words. I was keenly aware of the palpable presence of God's divine love within my heart. In fact, I noticed how this divine love was actually fueling my very being. Each day at L'Arche I found myself spending my life with increased delight because I could feel the Father's continued effort to transform my heart. I felt more Christlike through the weakening of my pride as I grew in the humility of working with such vulnerable and loving people. Indeed, the labor could be quite challenging, and there were parts of the ministry that were very trying, but my lasting memory is a very loving one.

What was rising up within my prayer was profound gratitude for the power of this word of God's love, which I could sense speaking to my heart throughout those days. At L'Arche, I felt loved. I could detect that I was growing in my ability to love many people who did not have the capacity to communicate in spoken language—yet I could hear the loving voice of God responding to me through them and their brokenness in a beautiful and mysterious way. I loved that this was happening, and I loved that I was aware of this while it was occurring.

In my prayer, I found my heart returning to the particular articulation of this truth that Maya Angelou had described in the book I stumbled upon a few weeks earlier in Denver. My love for those words had increased because the experience I was having in Toronto seemed to validate them increasingly each day. I had the strong sense that it was no coincidence that the power of this word had been given to me near the end of the retreat, as if I had been sealed in divine love and sent out into the world to help in its healing.

When I prayed over these feelings, I noticed a profound desire to meet this person whom God had enabled to speak so articulately what I was experiencing interiorly. In my prayer I sensed that the Father was inviting me to find Maya Angelou on my pilgrimage. I was coming to recognize in prayer that the upcoming pilgrim destination wasn't going to be a place but rather, it would be a person. While I was in Toronto, this desire only seemed to grow stronger in my prayer.

So, on those days off in Toronto, I visited the public library a few times. The librarians in both suburban Richmond Hill, where our L'Arche community was, and in Toronto were helpful as I began to research contact information for Maya Angelou. My strategy was to write to her and see if I might arrange a meeting sometime in the coming months during the pilgrimage. Remember, this was during pre-Internet 1994. All I knew was that she was the Reynolds Professor of American Studies at Wake Forest University in Winston-Salem, North Carolina.

Over the next few weeks, from libraries in Canada and also in Saint Paul, Minnesota, I was able to find three different addresses that looked potentially helpful. To each of these I sent a copy of a letter describing my proposal. I didn't hear anything back the first time; I would find a new potential lead and then resend the same letter to the new address. In fact, I still have a letter I had written to her after the pilgrimage, returned to sender, unopened from 1994, which I carry with me in my prayer book. I think it is a Christmas card I sent to her, but I don't remember.

Our experiment in Toronto lasted for two months, and then we returned to Minnesota, where we had a reunion with our other classmates. We remained at the novitiate for a short period of rest, during which began the discerning conversations with the novice master about the pilgrimage experiment. Remember, a Jesuit is always *sent* on his mission—we don't make our own assignments. After prayer and conversations with our superiors we trust that God works through the leadership of our religious community and that the Father speaks to us through the superior, from whom we receive a particular mission. Those novice experiments were a foretaste of a lifetime of being sent on Jesuit missions.

For the pilgrimage experiment each novice is sent out of the community for six weeks with $30 cash and a one-way bus ticket. He is to survive by begging. The whole point of the experiment is to receive a very special grace of profound trust that the Father will always provide, precisely through the kindness and generosity of other people.

Pilgrimage is a time of tremendous vulnerability and absolute dependence upon the Holy Spirit at work through one's fellow men and women. In the Jesuits' *Constitutions*, Saint Ignatius described the experiment as a way "to grow accustomed to discomfort in food and lodging" and that the novice, "through abandoning all the reliance which he could have in money or other created things, may with genuine faith and intense love place his reliance entirely in his Creator and Lord." It was to be an experiment of profound trust in God's providence.

In those preparatory conversations that occurred after we returned to Saint Paul from the hospital experiment, the novice master described for us the goals of the upcoming pilgrimage. It was important that we have time to ponder these goals before beginning our journey so that we would have them in mind as we made our way as pilgrims. In hindsight, I know that this actually was our introduction to lifelong Jesuit ideals, the seeds of which were being planted in the novice experiments. While they were specific to the experiment itself, they were, in reality, desires that the Jesuit would strive to fulfill during the future course of his life. The ultimate desire, it seemed to me, was that we were to view the entirety of human life as a pilgrimage, the destination ultimately being the eternal life of heaven. Along the way God would provide great gifts of friendship, marvelous opportunities, and profound challenges. This experiment would be a six-week microcosm of what we were to experience through the whole of life.

Father Pat McCorkell outlined for us the specific goals the Jesuits had in mind for us as we ventured forth. He gave us points to consider for the important preparation time that would help us as we discerned our pilgrimage.

- We were to pray for a deeper trust in God's providential care and our utter dependence upon God while we were on mission.

- We were to foster in our hearts the virtue of hope for the surprises in store for us, because a pilgrim was to believe that God's generosity was more than sufficient for whatever we would need.

- We were to seek the opening of our hearts and minds to transformation, so that through our dependency upon those we would meet, we might more easily identify with those who are poor and needy in other ways.

- We were to anticipate what it might be like to experience "discomfort in food and lodging" and to refine our ability to adapt to whatever circumstances in which we found ourselves.

- We were to grow in our service of the church to discover the capacity for initiative and creativity for the ministries of Catholicism.

- We were to seek the Father's desire for our ongoing discernment and choice of ministries.

- We were to celebrate our potential for formation as future apostles. The experience of pilgrimage would energize us in working with others for future ministries by pointing out emerging talents and spiritual gifts. It was to be a time of profound revelation.

- Through critical analysis of our culture, we would grow in our ability to hear interiorly what the Father hoped for each of us in our contribution to the world and its ongoing transformation into the kingdom of God.

- Through the continued integration of the graces we received while praying the Spiritual Exercises, we were to be receptive to vocational confirmation that the Father was calling us to live as Jesuits, as contemplatives in action.

Father Pat wanted us to be mindful of Jesus' instruction for the disciples as they were sent out for the proclamation of the gospel, as described in the tenth chapter of the Gospel of Matthew: "Whatever town or village you go into, ask for someone trustworthy and stay with them until you leave."

There were other elements to keep in mind as we journeyed, many touching on the human formation that the pilgrimage sought to facilitate, especially anything arising from the inevitable encounters with spiritual and actual poverties. Before we ventured forth, Father Pat wanted us to be aware of the potential challenges and opportunities that the coming weeks would provide. They could contain some of our hidden strengths, fears, and vulnerabilities. Only through taking time to examine them prayerfully would we be able to detect the hand of God at work.

We might expect to experience what he called interrelational poverty—not being known and not knowing those we would encounter on the journey. This would expose us to some chaos and lack of control, and we were to pay attention to what these conditions caused to surface within our hearts. There was also the reality of the poverty of being alone for those weeks without anything familiar and, conversely, poverty within human relationships if we were to be sent on pilgrimage with a Jesuit companion. A novice could feel quite isolated on pilgrimage and he could experience a lack of privacy. Courage, fortitude, and perseverance were the virtues he was to call upon in the face of these dimensions of poverty.

There was also the social dimension of the pilgrimage. Father Pat hoped it would provide the opportunity to grow in our sensitive awareness of what it means to be homeless, hungry, and without support. This exposure would help us grow closer to Christ by encouraging us to be compassionate and generous to people in need we would meet in the future. It would also help us overcome pride so that our future selves would be receptive to and dependent upon generosity when we found ourselves in need.

Ideally, this would yield a deeper appreciation of life's simple necessities, such as food, shelter, and belonging. Our capacity to grow in such appreciation for the basics would contribute to a deepening of our gratitude for life and our sense of the justice we would promote throughout our lives.

During those preparatory days the novice master gave us directives for the upcoming pilgrimage. We were expected to telephone the novitiate about once every week to ten days to stay bonded with the community and to help the staff monitor where we were and how we were doing. We were instructed to give away any excess of alms that we received. We were to make an effort to visit the churches in the places we visited and to pray for the people of those communities and to join in their celebration of the Eucharist. We were asked to keep a journal and to refrain from contacting or seeking any support from family and friends unless there were overriding unusual circumstances.

Beyond this general preparation, we needed to discern the specific destinations and then be "missioned" to them. Father Pat was happy to listen to our desires, and I shared with him my hope of finding Maya Angelou and the efforts I had already made to contact her. He was a bit hesitant about my being sent toward North Carolina without having received any responses to my letters of inquiry. While there is little that can be controlled during the pilgrimage itself, I think he wanted to make certain there was at least some receptivity from Maya Angelou. Before he would send me, he advised me to contact Wake Forest University by phone.

I remember going to the library in Saint Paul and finding a phone number to what I think was the English department at Wake Forest. When I placed the call, I am quite sure the secretary thought I was a complete fool or a crazy stalker—probably both. I imagine that on the receiving end it must have been an absolutely bizarre conversation. I explained who I was and that I was to be sent on a pilgrimage, arriving on a one-way bus ride from Minnesota with $30 cash and that I was hoping to come to Wake Forest to see Maya Angelou and . . . might I schedule an appointment to see her? Perhaps lunch? . . . Or dinner? I didn't drink coffee.

I wonder what must have been going through the secretary's mind as she listened to me. All I remember is a significant pause on the phone after my meandering and awkward request. She said quite forcefully that I wouldn't be seeing Dr. Angelou. My response to her dismissal included something like "the novice master needs to know if the poet will see me."

"What is a novice master? Who is this? Is this some kind of a joke?"

Well, I was a bit persistent and in a moment of frustration I remember her saying something to the effect of Maya Angelou being an extremely busy and popular person and that she didn't see people who popped by for a chat. I told her that I needed to know if I would be received, and she said no. She must have thought I was a total nut.

I told her that the one-way-ticket destination needed to be decided soon, and I asked her if I could give it a try and come to Wake Forest. She said something like, "If I were you, I wouldn't even try it. It isn't going to happen."

The following day I told the novice master that they knew I was coming!

This was true, but I suppose it was also a bit of a stretch. I didn't tell him the details.

My classmate Mark and I were given one-way Greyhound bus tickets to Knoxville, Tennessee. If I remember correctly, it was about a twenty-four-hour bus ride from Saint Paul. We left on Tuesday, April 19, 1994. We were sent out with a letter from the novice master addressed "To Whom This May Concern." If we were ever questioned about what we were doing, we would be able to prove our legitimacy by presenting a letter that contained contact information for the Jesuit novitiate and an explanation of what we were doing. We were missioned to begin our pilgrimage on the Appalachian Trail and to see how God would provide for us from that starting point.

3

Of Men and Mice

We left the Greyhound bus dazed and confused after such a long
time sitting. When we left Minnesota, nothing was green—the rem-
nant of a long, gray winter season. From the vantage point of a large
Greyhound window, however, I noticed the world becoming more
alive as we moved southward on the journey. The grass was green-
ing, and I was delighted when we first encountered blossoming trees
as we went through Cincinnati. This new springtime gave me hope
as we continued our journey toward Tennessee.

The arrival in Knoxville was quite frustrating. I was tired, hot,
and cranky from the long bus ride. My eyes ached from wearing contact lenses for so many hours, and the hair fairy had paid a special
visit to me while I dozed on the bus. We stood outside the depot
in the heat and tried to get our bearings, for we had no idea where
we were or where we could go. After asking directions from people on the street, we walked from the depot to a Catholic church
run by the Paulists, a Catholic community of priests. They sent us
to the University of Tennessee—where the Paulists also staffed the
Catholic Newman Center. The priests were unavailable at that time,
so we continued walking in the city, searching for someplace to rest.
Compared to Minnesota, it was quite hot outside—probably over
eighty degrees —and we certainly felt the change in climate. I felt

increasingly deflated as we continued to wander aimlessly without any success. It seemed that not a single person wanted to help us. It was our first moment of real need, and I remember feeling embarrassed by my neediness. Because we were new pilgrims, it was hard to approach people and ask them for help. It hadn't even been a full day, and I already felt like a total failure as a pilgrim. I know that sounds crazy, but I was exhausted and afraid because it was all so new to me. We simply needed a place to sleep and have a chance to bathe.

Eventually we made our way to the Holy Ghost Catholic Church on the outskirts of town, where we met an elderly priest who spoke to us only through a screened door. When we began to explain that we were pilgrims, he wouldn't have any of it. He dismissed us quickly and said we'd have better luck getting help at the Salvation Army in town than from him!

We worked our way back to the university. When we arrived, a young student named Stephen was compassionate toward us. Sensing our fatigue and discouragement, he was going to arrange for us to stay with his parents—at least to use their shower and have a place to sleep before we entered the Appalachian Trail. At that very moment, however, the priests at the Newman Center returned, and they were instantly helpful. One of them, Father Stan MacNevin, brought us to the residence of John XXIII Parish and allowed us to bathe and rest there—and then he took the two of us out for some dinner. He was profoundly kind and welcoming. When we told him about the pilgrimage and our intention to enter the Appalachian Trail, he showed immediate concern. He warned that night in the woods would be very cold. He didn't think it wise for us to be out in the mountains; he observed correctly that we had very little equipment with us. I had a backpack; inside it were contact lens solution and glasses, a razor, a toothbrush and paste, a pair of boots, two pairs of underwear, two T-shirts, two pairs of socks, a pair of pants, shorts, a bandana, a sweatshirt, a blanket, a journal, a rosary, a jar of peanut butter, a water bottle, some crackers, a deck of cards, and half a roll of toilet paper.

When we woke up the next morning, it was clear that Father Stan's concern for us had deepened during the night, for he tried again to talk us out of going onto the trail. When he saw that we were determined, he insisted that we allow him at least to drive us to the entrance. We agreed to this kind offer, and when we went out to the car, we found that he had packed an additional blanket for each of us. On the way, he pulled into a grocery store and insisted that we allow him to purchase some food for our journey. We picked only a few things; we both felt that he had already been immensely generous. Soon we were driving past Dollywood, and then we arrived at the entrance to Great Smoky Mountains National Park, a magnificent but small part of the entire Appalachian Trail. As we exited his car, Father Stan told us that he believed we were crazy and we could be assured that he would be praying for us on our journey. We left filled with profound gratitude for his kindness toward us. I am sure we inconvenienced him a great deal with such an unexpected visit, but this good priest made us feel as if we were the most important item on his agenda for the day. When I think of the University of Tennessee and our experience with the people we met there, I'm filled with fond gratitude.

Our first day in the Smoky Mountains involved a six-mile hike. The contrast of what twenty-four hours contained boggled my mind. A day earlier I would have done anything to get out of the bus to stretch my legs. Now, after a few hours on the trail, I found myself longing for a chair.

We discovered that at least on this section of the trail, there were shelters where hikers spent the night. They were basic: small three-sided structures with long wooden planks for people to sleep on. The front side was open air. At our first night's shelter we were in the company of two others—a twenty-five-year-old man from Australia named Lyndon, and John, a fifty-one-year-old man from the United States who had recently lost his lumber purchasing job. My initial impression was that shelter life would prove awkward. There wasn't much conversation when we arrived in the evening, but as the sun went down, we started a little campfire and began to chat. My earlier impression quickly changed. These two men provided a warm introduction to life on the trail. They had met while they were hiking a few days earlier, and like many individuals on the trail, they decided to walk together until they eventually parted ways to meet others along the path. They both intended to hike the entire trail, beginning at Springer Mountain in Georgia and traveling through fourteen states before ending at Mount Katahdin in Maine: 2,181 miles.

What I learned from John that evening was that all sorts of people come to the trail for all sorts of reasons. Many find themselves in the midst of significant change in life. It was his observation that people turn to nature to help them discover a deeper and more sincere interiority. It seems that the journey of the trail provides access to the courage people need to pursue greater freedom. In that evening conversation we learned that in his unemployment, John felt the freedom to be able to do something he had always wanted to do but had never given himself the permission to pursue. Once work was taken away, he wondered, *Without a job, who am I?* He shared with us that on the trail his reflections upon that question helped him realize that his work had become too self-defining and that he was in reality much more than his labor. He had been living as if the opposite were true.

Lyndon talked about the struggle as he grew into his midtwenties. He realized that he hadn't yet discerned his vocation. The sublime surroundings of the Appalachian Trail and the quiet reflection were enabling him to find encouragement as he hiked through these mountains. He realized that there were bigger, more meaningful questions in life but that his superficial lifestyle prevented him from examining them. He had been in university but left after three years because he wasn't certain about the purpose of his study. He hadn't discerned his deeper desires and found himself simply going through the motions of college life, partying away his real potential. Hiking the trail helped him in his pursuit of clarity and confidence. It gave him the opportunity for contemplative silence and meaningful conversation, which he was coming to understand as the means to discovering what he really wanted in life. Along the way he was learning that humans need other people who will listen to us and help us explore the greater questions of life. He described how it was increasingly apparent that this combination of deep reflection and conversation brought him great happiness and satisfaction as he continued along the way.

When we revealed to Lyndon and John that we were Jesuits who were studying to become Catholic priests, there was an abrupt change in the kind of conversation we were having, and I remember loving this transformative moment. Now each of us was free to talk more explicitly about God. The stillness of the surrounding Appalachian Mountains, visible through the flicker of a warm campfire, helped us to recognize that we were living in the midst of the beauty God created for us to enjoy. I can still remember clearly how I experienced just then a deep intimacy and satisfaction in this capacity to rest unabashedly in the presence of God, the one from whom all such good things come. This conversation took place underneath a magnificent starry sky. John and Lyndon loved the idea of the pilgrimage experience, and they thought it was wise for us to begin in a beautiful environment such as the Smoky Mountains.

During our conversation the sun had set, and although we had a small campfire, I was already very cold. We hadn't much to eat at all, and I could feel my body weakening from the exertion of the day's hike. Soon we were getting out our blankets and placing them on the wooden planks of the shelter. We were closing up our backpacks when Lyndon advised us to keep them open all night. He warned that if we zipped up the packs, the mice would eat through them.

The next day we hiked about ten miles through some very rugged terrain, and my feet were starting to blister. We passed the Mt. Collins shelter and soon approached Newfound Gap. Even though it was hot and sunny at that moment, I recalled Father Stan's warnings of cold nights and how I was already regretting not having some warmer clothes for the nighttime. I hadn't slept well the night before—mostly because I was cold. There was a parking lot for trail walkers at this place, and I wondered if I might run into someone who was beginning a day trip and who had extra clothing. There were a few people in the parking lot, and I approached them as a beggar would but came up empty-handed. As we continued on the trail, we encountered one day-hiker, a lady who had a sweatshirt around her waist. I asked her if I could have it. I think my request caught her off guard. She glanced at me quizzically, and I told her simply, "It's been very cold at night, and I don't have much warm clothing." She said no but that she had some sweatpants back in the parking lot. I thought the lot was too far back and I didn't want to interrupt her hike by having her return to her car.

She did tell me that she would pray for me and that I would be protected through the gift of prayer. She said this with sincerity and seriousness, and I liked that very much, because I am a strong believer in the gift of intercessory prayer.

Then she chuckled as she untied the sweatshirt around her waist to show it to me and said, "Prayer is better. You wouldn't have wanted this." I looked down at the sweatshirt in her hands. I don't recall specifically what the design was—my memory sees something like a gigantic Hello Kitty and the word "Grandma" on it. Over all these years what remains clearly with me to this day is that I was grateful for that promise of prayer and that this warm little exchange in the midst of those beautiful mountains fortified my trust in prayer.

Then we descended a rugged portion of the trail for about four miles in a marvelously beautiful section of the Appalachians. The terrain was uneven, and I was thirsty and unstable with my footing—I wiped out a couple of times. We arrived at Kephart shelter and nobody was around—our first shelter without other hikers!

I thought that this would be my favorite shelter. Everything about it was lovely. There was a waterfall behind the shelter, and I was already looking forward to sleeping with that constant crash of water in the background. We gathered firewood, and I washed my socks and underwear in that cold stream and tended to the blisters on my feet. As the sun began to set, we sat in front of a small campfire eating our dinner. We planned to sleep on the ground near the fire to stay warm that night; it was already cold. The fire diminished, and we prepared ourselves for the night.

As soon as we were wrapped in our blankets, things changed abruptly.

I felt the first one on my head and thought it was simply the breeze. As I started to doze, I felt the second one zip across my face, brushing just beneath my nostrils.

Mice.

We both sat up quickly and realized that mice were all over the campsite. My heart was pounding, and I thought I might vomit! But there was nothing to be done. There was no place to go, nobody to call. This was simply what life was bringing to us in that moment and we were not in charge. So we tied bandanas over our mouths and noses in such a way that the cloth also covered our ears. I will never forget that night of mice running across my face, darting through my blanket—and me shivering both from the cold and from my disgust at those nasty little critters scampering around my body. It was a fitful night, and I kept thinking of Ignatius's desire that we experience "discomfort in food and lodging." This experience seemed to fulfill that goal.

On Saturday we were at Pecks Corner, a shelter about ten miles farther along the trail. We were both exhausted—sleep deprived, sore, and running low on food. This shelter was quite full with nine people. I was grateful for this because if the mice were bad again, then at least there would be competition: seven other people for them to explore! The campers made a huge fire, and all of us had gathered wood from the forest so we knew this fire would last into the night. As people sat for their dinner, Mark and I went around to them and begged for anything extra they might have. This was my first experience of begging for food on the trail. We were hesitant to do this because we knew that hikers are very careful about the provisions they pack; they want to carry only what they need. To ask for "extra" would imply that they weren't precise packers, which could be insulting to hikers who had carefully planned their journeys. Our asking for food would mean that they sacrifice some of their well-calculated provisions.

Well, the people we met at this site were marvelous—and it didn't take us long to become good friends. When they learned we were Jesuit pilgrims in need of food, they immediately came to our assistance. We received noodle mixes, pieces of bread, and mashed-potato powder, and one new friend named Sheryl, who was from Connecticut, introduced us to ramps, something like wild onions, which we could find on the trail and cook and eat.

As we sat around that campfire, I told one man, "Mountain Bob" from Georgia, that we'd had mouse problems the night before. His pragmatic reply: "No pain. No rain. No Maine." Such things were to be expected if we continued the journey. Keeping the goal in mind would help us face any difficulty along the way. Goals serve to motivate us and remind us of why we are doing what we are doing. Mountain Bob was a "through" hiker who had his sights set on Mount Katahdin. He was also a bit strange—his pack weighed over a hundred pounds, and in it were items we thought quite unusual to carry such a distance, including a large bellow for the fire. Why he brought this I do not know, but as that night's campfire was the best we'd had so far, I wasn't going to ask questions.

When it came time to settle down for the night, people started to put away their gear and ready their sleeping bags. To prevent another night of cold, I developed a new strategy. I noticed one man wearing a sweatshirt at the campfire. As he prepared his plank for sleeping, I complimented him on that nice sweatshirt. He thanked me, and then I said, "I bet it keeps you nice and warm. May I sleep with it?" He started laughing and handed it to me. I told him I'd return it in the morning. I slept well, though there was a large man from Indiana on the plank next to me who snored constantly. I felt as if I were in the midst of a lumber mill, lying on that plank and listening to him snore-sawing through the night. I would nudge him occasionally to get him to stop, but a moment later he would start again. My nudges soon became slight pushes, which evolved into shoves and then blossomed into quick, deliberate punches. I would give him a quick hit and then immediately turn to the other side and pretend to sleep, but none of this seemed to matter.

In the morning I returned the sweatshirt to my new friend. As people ate their small breakfasts, they commented on the night of sleep. The man from Indiana complained that his side was sore from the night. "It must have been from sleeping on that cold, wooden plank," said one of the others.

My classmate and I rolled up our blankets and left the shelter to start our hike for the day. I enjoyed this larger group immensely and found myself feeling sad as we departed, because we didn't know how far the others were planning to hike that day. The two of us decided to make a shorter hike, and when we arrived at the Tri-Corner Knob shelter, some of the great people we had met the night before soon followed: Vern, Mike, Sheryl, and Ryan and Rebecca, a father and daughter from the state of Maine. Sheryl was thirty-one years old and had been in recovery from alcoholism for over six years. I didn't understand exactly what had brought her to the Appalachian Trail, but I found her to be a kind and supportive person. A small group of us was playing the card game UNO by the campfire that evening. In a quiet moment Sheryl shared with us a reflection that she turned to for strength each day in her ongoing recovery. I found what she shared to be helpful as I grew into the identity of a pilgrim, because it seemed to be true to my own unfolding experience.

> Picture yourself walking through a meadow. There is a path opening before you. As you walk, you feel hungry. Look to your left. There's a fruit tree in full bloom. Pick what you need.
>
> Steps later, you notice you're thirsty. On your right, there's a fresh water spring.
>
> When you are tired, a resting place emerges. When you are lonely, a friend appears to walk with you. When you get lost, a teacher with a map appears.
>
> Before long, you notice the flow: need and supply; desire and fulfillment. Maybe, you wonder, Someone gave me the need because Someone planned to fulfill it. Maybe I had to feel the need, so I would notice and accept the gift. Maybe closing my eyes to the desire closes my arms to its fulfillment.

Demand and supply, desire and fulfillment—a continuous cycle, unless we break it. All the necessary supplies have already been planned and provided for this journey.

Today, everything I need shall be supplied to me.[1]

When Sheryl finished sharing this, we were silent, all eyes upon the warm, bright campfire before us. My heart and mind were resting in the truth Sheryl had offered us. Here we were in the middle of the mountains of North Carolina, sitting with a bunch of strangers who were literally sharing their food and the clothes off their backs. In my view, God was bringing me into contact with excellent people who were caring and supportive and who wanted to share with me their own experiences of life's journey. Everything I needed was being provided. All I needed to do was trust that God's hand was at work. It was so simple! I felt energized and hopeful.

As the fire began to die down, some of the others stepped away from it, and then Sheryl stood up to stretch, for we had been sitting on tree logs around the campfire the whole time. She announced quietly to us that she was going to put on a log dance. I didn't know what this was, but I thought maybe it was something special that people from Connecticut did while they were camping, so when she went to the shelter to prepare, I called the rest of the group to come over and announced that Sheryl was going to put on a log dance for us. As the group reassembled around the fire, she returned, but there was no dance. I had misheard her. She had actually said that she was going to put on long pants.

So much for our night of campfire entertainment.

My announcement yielded a rather awkward moment for everyone who had gathered eagerly around the fire; they quietly returned to the shelter, disappointed. They went to bed, but Mark and I

---

1. Melody Beattie, *The Language of Letting Go: Daily Meditations on Codependency* (Center City, MN: Hazelden Foundation, 1990), March 29.

remained by the fire, mostly because I felt so foolish! The moon was so full and bright, and the sky was packed with stars, even with that bright moon. Despite my being embarrassed, I could still discern that it was a beautiful, chilly evening.

The next morning we began what would be our longest hike yet; we traveled more than fourteen miles and arrived at Davenport Gap, which was almost straight downhill. My legs were sore from the pounding of the descent, but the scenery of those stunning Smoky Mountains made my aches disappear. We often found our-selves pausing along the way simply to gaze out at the magnificent landscape in front of us, which I experienced as the grandeur of God's creation. When we arrived at Davenport, the real treat of the day was yet to come. Our friends from the previous two nights had decided to make the long journey as well, foregoing earlier shelters in order to join us at Davenport. It was a great reunion filled with stories, shared food, marvelous conversation, and warm friendship.

Around the fire that evening, the depth of our sharing centered on the experience of being young and the challenges that faced our generation. In my recollection, the issues centered upon decision making and the fear of choosing wrongly. We were in complete agreement that as young Americans we were living in a period of tremendous abundance and opportunity. In fact, several of our trail friends revealed that they were hiking simply because they felt over-whelmed with good choices for the future and they felt stuck. They had come to the woods to discern what they believed to be a more sincere and authentic desire for the mysterious next step of their lives. They wanted to learn to choose wisely. The question: How to go about doing that?

For me, answering that question comes down to prayer, sincerity, and mentoring. Part of what had drawn this group of hikers to the Appalachian Trail was the desire for contemplative silence. When a person is in the midst of the grandeur of such beautiful creation, she or he finds an increased capacity for deeper reflection. I think humans need both interior and exterior space to ponder the big questions in life. When a person's surroundings contain the depth of beauty, it seems that he or she will have a greater ability to receive the desired clarity and peace. The perspective that nature provides from regular life provides refreshment and new vision. In such an environment a person of faith begins to ponder the reality of the living God. For many people, being in the midst of creation opens the heart to a relationship with God. It is a breakthrough moment to recognize that you can speak directly to God, and this relationship is what is called prayer.

In this process of pondering and discovering possibilities for the future, it seems that vulnerability and sincerity are of crucial importance. I have come to appreciate the pursuit of sincerity, and I turn to it often with great affection as I examine how I'm living and loving the gift of life. At the end of the day, I often ask God to show me when I have been most sincere during the day and when sincerity has been lacking within me.

There is a popular etymology that understand the word *sincere* to mean, literally, to be "without wax." My understanding is that the word *sincere* comes from the artistic world. I can imagine a sculptor standing in front of a large block of marble. As she is chipping away, creating her work of art, perhaps the marble fractures in a way that she didn't intend. The artist might be tempted to fill in that break with wax so that the casual onlooker doesn't notice the fracture. The astute art critic, however, would recognize that this work is not sincere; it is "with wax."

The best art is always sincere, without wax. A sincere creator learns to integrate everything that has occurred in the process of her creation, so that in the long term nothing is viewed as perpetually burdensome and therefore needing to be covered or hidden. That's the point of integration; it embraces what has occurred in the past so that nothing is viewed as forever shameful, mistaken, repulsive, or embarrassing.

Christians believe that every human being is a work of God, that each person has been made by the Father *sincerely* and, in his eyes, *completely*. Perhaps the greatest damage to a human life occurs when a person feels that the creator hasn't done an adequate job, that somehow the honest limitations and imperfections that come with being human equal deficit, major failure, and unworthiness, especially when a person compares him- or herself with the supposed perfection of others. This kind of self-perception is a lie and must be dismissed.

In hindsight, I can tell that what united our community of hikers on the Appalachian Trail was our vulnerable, reflective conversation. There was no pretense among us. What I felt as my own complete acceptance of all the others was reciprocated—I felt completely accepted by them, and this was lovely, indeed. Sincerity was the fruit of such thoughtful and heartfelt exchange.

In the woods, there wasn't a single person to impress. No one cared about status—neither one's own nor that of the people met along the way. The adventure wasn't about credentials, cars, or clothes. In the woods, what you see is what you get!

What impressed me most was the goodness of the people I encountered. We were in the midst of pilgrims who were on the way, people who were seeking a greater good for the future. It remains curious to me that I could be sitting on a subway car in Boston with these same people without exchanging a single word or even making eye contact. I wonder what it was about the woods that provided the freedom to meet one another.

It seems to me that there's a temptation along the pilgrim way to feel that the journey is meant to be lonesome and solitary. Isn't a person supposed to figure out everything by him- or herself? Sometimes the journey can feel like this, but it doesn't need to be this way. Mentoring can be quite important on the journey. It is a gift to be able to ponder the future while looking to the example of others who are well along the journey of life, those who inspire us by the way they live. It is good to listen to them and ask them questions about what they have seen and what they have learned. Pride makes a person feel that he should not seek advice or good counsel. On our journey along the Appalachian Trail, we depended on the insights of those who had gone before us. At that time on the trail, people left journals at the shelters, and hikers would spend time reflecting on their experiences at a particular shelter or part of the trail. For example, some people noted in the journal if and where they had spotted wildlife. (We wrote about our experience with the mice in that shelter's journal!) I liked that the advice was there for the taking; I could choose to read it or not to read it.

I have found that more often than not, the mentoring I have received has been instrumental in helping me find my way. In the Society of Jesus, this has been a gift of crucial importance. I love to consult with others, to run ideas by them, to ask their impressions. I do this because there are people I love who know me in ways that I do not know myself. They are often the people who live in ways that I greatly admire. Their perspective is immensely helpful because, fundamentally, the art of mentoring is the handing on of wisdom. Wisdom is the fruit of human experience examined and shared, and each generation depends on receiving the accumulated wisdom passed along from that generation's elders.

On our final night on the trail, Ryan, Rebecca's dad, told us that being on the Appalachian Trail makes a person look at himself. "You can't get away from you because you're all you've got." I think there was some wisdom transmitted there. While going and growing along the way, a person must be at home with himself, sincerely. If I detect insincerity in myself, the journey provides many opportunities for me to shed it.

The next morning we exited the trail and went to Mountain Mama's, where I ate a huge cheeseburger for breakfast. It was my first time in North Carolina, and I wanted to stop camping and to make our way toward Wake Forest University. I felt that the trail had served its purpose for the beginning of the pilgrimage. I was itching to get going because I was sunburned, stinking, and satisfied with what we had experienced in the woods. Yet we really enjoyed the trail, and we were tempted to continue in the mountains. We were at a crossroads of sorts, for we were close to Interstate 40. We debated whether to head back onto the trail or walk along the highway. This was an important decision. After a moment of prayerful silence, we decided to trust that whatever needed to happen would happen. Thus far, God had provided good people and the splendor of creation. There were no indications that this would cease to be true at Mountain Mama's.

4

Sweet Carolina

Mark and I were standing outside Mountain Mama's after our burger breakfast, deliberating whether to walk to the interstate or head back to the Appalachian Trail. It was obvious from our backpacks and our lack of bathing during the past week that we had been on the trail. A man approached us and asked us to tell him about our hike. After we gave him a brief report, he told us he'd gladly give us a ride to Waynesville, which was about twenty miles from Asheville. With this unexpected offer, it seemed that our decision about whether or not to continue on the trail had been made for us. Seeing this offer as a sudden opportunity, we trusted that it was divine providence. We jumped in his truck and rode with him, chatting about the beautiful Smoky Mountains as we rushed past them. It was easier driving through them than walking!

When we arrived in Waynesville, he dropped us off on the interstate, and we started walking on that highway to Asheville. About twenty minutes later, another truck stopped for us. The driver, who introduced himself as Mountain Bob (perhaps a common name on the Appalachian Trail, given our campfire starter!), offered to drive us the rest of the way to Asheville. My impression was that Mountain Bob found us to be simultaneously offensive, smelly, and curious, which I found to be funny, for he had a mouthful of tobacco that was leaking juice down his chin. He asked that we sit in the bed of his pickup, which we did, and then he zipped us down the interstate toward the city. I was freezing because of the wind whipping us as we cruised down the highway, but I recall looking at those mountains, with sun and spring in the air, and experiencing an overwhelming sense of gratitude. All along the way through those mountains we had received direction and care.

As we came into Asheville, Mountain Bob pulled into the parking lot of a restaurant. The initials on the restaurant sign were HH, but I don't remember its specific name. As we stood in the parking lot, Bob announced that he wanted us to hang out with him for the day. He took out a boom box and put it in the bed of the truck and started to play some loud music, asking us if we were Grateful Dead fans. Then he wanted us to go to his brother's house for a shower and then to smoke some weed! Well, this wasn't really how I wanted to spend the day, and the whole thing began to seem off. We thanked him for the ride and for his kindness, and he let up and drove away.

So here we were: Asheville, North Carolina. I felt strangely out of place in this new environment, for we were in the presence of cars instead of trees. Clearly, we were out of the woods. What to do? This was different territory that required a new pilgrim way of proceeding—it wouldn't be like showing up at a shelter on the Appalachian Trail and being in the presence of fellow hikers. Without the communion of the trail, how would we connect with other people? I felt a bit of a panic. What if I ended up standing in this parking lot for four weeks?

Mark went into the restaurant to look up the address of the Greyhound bus station in Asheville. The novice master had included in our provisions a bus ticket from Asheville to Winston-Salem. We needed to figure out how to get to the bus station. We weren't sure if we could use the tickets immediately, and we wondered if it would be wise for us to remain in Asheville for a while.

I stood outside the restaurant and waited for Mark, who suddenly called to me that I should come into the restaurant. His smile reassured me that some of the tension regarding our situation had just been resolved. Four retired men sat at a table. A moment earlier, when they saw Mark at the counter studying the phone book, they had started to chat with him. After they heard a bit about who we were and what we were doing, these guys wanted to buy us lunch and then drive us to the bus depot!

They quickly added another table to theirs. They treated us like sons who had returned to their fathers after a long journey away. They wanted to know all about our experience on the trail, what the weather had been like for us, and whether we stayed healthy the entire time. They were so encouraging and engaging! I was struck by this instant and magnificent kindness—it was the first of many amazing exchanges I had with the people of the great state of North Carolina.

After our lunch, two of these men drove us to the depot to see if we could use our bus tickets, which had been issued originally in Saint Paul to be used a couple of days later. The novice master wasn't sure how long we would spend or where we would end up on the Appalachian Trail. I suppose he provided this additional bus voucher as a backup in case we got into trouble and needed help getting to Winston-Salem. Earlier, when we were in Minnesota, none of us had any idea what the circumstances of the pilgrimage would be. Father Pat just wanted to do whatever he could to keep us safe and moving as best we could at the beginning of the journey. At the Asheville bus station, we received good news: we could use the tickets that evening. The Greyhound agent simply reissued them with a corrected date. Our kind friends arranged for our backpacks to be held at the station for our later retrieval, and then they invited us back into the car and drove us all around Asheville. They loved their city and told us all about it. They dropped us off near the Basilica of Saint Lawrence, a magnificent church. Neither of them were Catholic, but they loved this place and knew it would be important for us to see it. I don't know how they endured being in the same car with us, because we stunk so badly from our days in the wilderness. When they left us at the basilica, these two embraced us warmly and promised to pray for us as we continued our pilgrimage.

Mark and I stood in this magnificent basilica, a confluence of awe in our hearts, both for the beauty of the sanctuary in which we stood and for the gift of humanity God had just revealed through our new Asheville friends.

I crawled into a pew and knelt down. In the silence of that great church I prayed for the people of Asheville, especially for George and the others who had been so kind to us. Where did they come from? Why did they care for us in such a profound way? We showed up out of nowhere, and it seemed as if they had been waiting there at the diner for us the whole time, anticipating our arrival. They treated us affectionately, like family.

After our prayer we walked through the basilica to admire its beauty. We left and then went into a bookstore nearby, simply passing the time before our bus ride. I thought we would have been kicked out because of our appearance, but we were greeted with smiles and hellos.

Immediately at the entrance to this little bookstore was a table display featuring Maya Angelou's new book—which I had last seen in Denver. Upon encountering it, I felt my heart make a little leap. I perceived this as a divine confirmation and no mere coincidence—it was the Father's will for me to be in North Carolina. I felt a surge of confidence that I was on the right pilgrim path.

As I stood by the book display, I felt that God would be fortuitous to us at Wake Forest University. Perhaps it was because of the many graces we had already received on the pilgrimage—the hospitality at the University of Tennessee, the sublimity of the Appalachian Trail and the solidarity of fellow hikers, the kindness of the people of Asheville, the beauty of the basilica. As I stood at this display in this little bookstore, tears of deep gratitude welled up; it was a moment of direct communication and confirmation from the Father.

I picked up Angelou's text and reread the passage on the Power of the Word that had moved my heart so deeply a few months earlier in Denver. "God loves me."

It is true, I heard the Lord speak to my heart. And I knew that I was going to meet this poet because she could articulate what I was feeling at that precise moment.

Then Mark and I walked to the public library to research potential connections in Winston-Salem. Another visit to a library's phone-book collection. I know such dependence upon phone books sounds funny today, with the existence of the Internet, but this was just prior to its entrance into the public mainstream. Phone books were my research resource in 1994, and while that is kind of strange to admit, I remember my pilgrim heart being grateful for access to those phone books.

I met a reference librarian who brought me right away to the collection of phone books. For some reason, I felt depressed when I began to look at the listings. It seemed awkward to be calling places and putting people on the spot—and to ask for immediate help for that very night. I would hesitate to do that even to my siblings. I feared being vulnerable and dependent upon people—perhaps an unfounded fear, given the experiences of kindness we had accumulated so far.

Maybe it was a flashback to poor experiences that resulted from the previous searches I had done in Toronto and Saint Paul, but I didn't feel very confident about gazing at these random phone-book listings. I suggested to Mark that we return to the basilica to find someone to help us. After all, we only needed someplace to sleep. I thought that maybe we should stay in Asheville and take time to clean up and regain our strength after having been in the woods.

We left the library feeling somewhat defeated and tired and then headed back to the basilica, where we found someone standing in the entranceway. While I don't recall the specifics, somehow this person sensed we were sheep without a shepherd and led us to the basilica office. We stood there feeling pathetic, and once again I was taken aback by how warmly and kindly we were treated, for we had found ourselves among gentle souls who wanted to do whatever they could to help us.

In that office was a friendly and caring priest. When he learned that we were headed to Winston-Salem and hoped to find shelter there, he and the secretary started to recall parishes in that area that might offer resources. When we mentioned that we were Jesuits, the priest looked at us with a big, happy smile. He remembered that an older Jesuit was stationed at a small parish in Winston-Salem. He reached for a booklet, the diocesan directory, and found that this Jesuit, Father Larry Hunt, was serving by himself at a small city parish called St. Benedict. He wrote down the phone number for us and allowed us to place a long-distance call to Father Hunt from the basilica office. The phone rang several times before an elderly voice answered. I started to feel nervous and with some hesitation introduced myself and told Father Hunt that we were two Jesuit pilgrim novices calling from the basilica in Asheville, and that we were arriving in Winston-Salem that night. We were hoping to stay with him for a short time, and would that be permissible? Father

Hunt was incredibly gracious during what I can only imagine was a strange, unexpected, and inconvenient phone conversation. Without even a pause he said we could stay with him and that he would warmly welcome the company of Jesuit brothers. Then I hung up the phone. In that rectory office all of us looked at one another in silence. The secretary looked at us—we were so grungy, sunburned, and smelly—and said, "Well, this'll be very interesting for him!"

I'm not sure what Father Hunt felt after that call, but when we boarded the Greyhound to Winston-Salem, neither Mark nor I felt very confident about our upcoming arrival. It felt embarrassing to be so dependent on other people, especially total strangers. Yet consistently we had been led to marvelously kind people willing to help us in any way.

We arrived at the Winston-Salem bus depot that night, exhausted. We had come off the trail that morning and still had not bathed. I took out the paper with the scribbled phone number on it and called St. Benedict the Moor Parish. The phone rang and rang, finally activating the answering machine. My immediate thought was that something had happened to complicate our fragile plan. The priest had forgotten about us. He smelled us over the phone and then changed his mind about our visit. He had already gone to bed and fallen asleep.

Then I listened to the prerecorded message. Father Hunt had created a message specifically for us—simply to reassure us that he was on his way to meet us at the bus station. We stood still for a bit, and then a kindly looking elderly man approached us and introduced himself as Larry Hunt. He shook our hands and embraced us as if we were his long-lost sons who had returned from a faraway journey. We got into his car, and he brought us back to the parish rectory, where he lived by himself. The house was a mess! The first thing he asked was whether we could cook, and when we said we could, he asked us to make a dinner for all of us to share. It was after ten o'clock!

Wearily we put down our bags and went to work putting together some chicken and pasta. I remember wondering if Fr. Hunt would have had anything for his dinner had we not shown up on the scene. In hindsight, I believe that this kind old priest delayed his dinner so that our late arrival would begin with the hospitality of a shared meal.

When we sat down to dinner, we soon discovered that Larry Hunt was not only a gracious host but also a very interesting Jesuit and an inspiring apostle. We learned that most of his active ministry had been in India, where he spent years and years working with and caring for a community of lepers. When he could no longer keep up with the demands of this work overseas, he returned to the United States and was sent to Winston-Salem to serve in this tiny parish all by himself. St. Benedict's was a poor Catholic parish, predominantly African American. We would learn from our attendance at the daily Mass that it was a parish of deep faith and joy. Each morning at St. Benedict's the same parishioners would come to celebrate the Eucharist and to pray for the intentions of their families. It was obvious to us that in his "retirement," Larry was still deeply devoted to the Jesuit mission—he was still of great service and generosity as he assisted the people of St. Martin in their spiritual needs. He had a gentle presence, and he welcomed Mark and me instantly and graciously, simply through the sharing of his ministry to the poor.

After our dinner and lengthy conversation, Larry excused us from the dining room and we were finally able to shave and clean up. In my memory of that night, the experience of taking a hot shower and then crawling into bed is among the more anticipated and satisfying moments in my twenty-three years of living. We were in good company and life was good, but perhaps even more important was that I recognized these truths right then and there. I fell asleep with a grateful, secure heart.

After a night of deep sleep, I attended Mass, and then Larry said he would drive me to Wake Forest University. Wake Forest was a beautiful campus—and it was large. I had no idea where to go or what to do. It was a mild spring morning, so after Larry dropped me off, I decided to sit on a campus bench to position myself and be ready to meet Maya Angelou. It was midmorning, and I think I arrived when students were already in class; the campus was very quiet. My short-term strategy was to remain seated on that bench and then when classes changed, approach students passing by and inquire as to who might know Maya Angelou. Maybe, I thought, Maya Angelou herself would walk by and I could invite her to join me for a coffee. So when students started coming and going, I mustered up enough courage to overcome my shyness and began asking random kids if they were in Maya Angelou's class that semester.

In hindsight, I understand that this strategy probably appeared to be quite strange and that many of the students I approached found my request to be awkward. I felt quite self-conscious, too, for as you can imagine, I was getting nowhere. The students were in a hurry, and I probably came across as an odd duck. Someone told me that Maya Angelou's office was in a particular building and pointed me in the direction of Wingate Hall. I went there and wandered inside Wingate until I stumbled across an office with her nameplate on the door.

I knocked. No answer. I asked the person across the hall if Dr. Angelou had office hours that day. Her reply: "I've never seen her at her office. I don't think she uses it." I then considered how perhaps this was a decoy office for strange people like me who showed up out of nowhere. That would make sense!

I returned to my bench, and when the next period occurred, I entered the center of a herd of passing students, thinking that someone in the group could help me. I met a student who recommended that I make my way to the Dean of the College.

I walked over to this office, and from the receptionist I learned that Maya Angelou had taken ill, so the course she had been teaching had concluded early. When I arrived, it was near the end of the semester; this change must have occurred while I was hiking the trail, for the secretary I'd talked to on the phone before leaving Saint Paul never mentioned that the class had ended.

So, Maya Angelou was no longer teaching. This was bad news indeed. This complicated things; I had been imagining that perhaps sometime during that week I would be able to sit in on her class and then maybe have a chance to chat with her either beforehand or afterward. But this new information brought instant deflation and confusion.

As I stood in the office taking this in, the assistant, Heidi Curtis, asked me if I was a university student. I said no, and when she asked what I was doing at Wake Forest, I explained briefly who I was and what I had hoped to do. Ms. Curtis appeared concerned and wanted to help. She said that looking for Maya Angelou on campus would be futile and that she never used her campus office—her real office was off campus. Actually, there were two off-campus offices, but they were unlisted. She went to her computer for a moment and then picked up the telephone. After some phone conversations, Heidi told me about a student at Wake Forest named Melissa Harris, who was particularly close to Maya Angelou—that some had known her on campus to be Angelou's protégée. Heidi wondered whether Melissa might be helpful for my quest.

Heidi telephoned Melissa. When Melissa didn't answer, Heidi left a voice message describing my situation. She asked that Melissa call the dean's office so that they might speak directly.

Then Heidi gave me Maya Angelou's real office phone number. We called and were told that Maya Angelou wasn't even in Winston-Salem at that moment.

As I was leaving the dean's office, Heidi handed me twenty dollars and asked that I call her the next day both to let her know how things were going and so that she could let me know if she had heard back from Melissa. Heidi Curtis was the kindest soul I met at Wake Forest. Her warmth, concern, and great efforts to help me were remarkable and inspiring.

When I left the dean's office, it was pouring rain. I caught up with Mark, and we waited and waited, but the rain did not let up, so we were forced to take a taxi because it was getting late and we had promised Larry that we would join him for dinner.

When we returned to the church, Larry told us that we would not be cooking. Instead, we were going to have dinner with some parishioners. We spent an evening at the home of Elsie and Clarence Nottingham, a pretty amazing couple. She was seventy-three years old, white, a former Philadelphia grade school teacher, and almost completely blind. Clarence was age ninety-one, black, originally from Harlem, and had a thriving career as a successful photographer. They shared a profound love for travel and had met a decade earlier while vacationing separately in Mexico. They developed a friendship while on their trip and eventually fell in love and were married. What seemed so interesting about them was that their love was clearly a union of completion. With her diminished vision, Elsie relied upon Clarence's guidance, and in his old age he needed her to help him with his daily routine. It was truly an example of marriage making two into one.

The Nottinghams were gracious hosts that evening, and we had a lovely time listening to their stories. Clarence shared some of his photography, which included magnificent scenes from his visits to Italy, as well as a sharp portrait he had taken of Martin Luther King Jr. Elsie shared with us that Clarence rarely shared his photography and his doing so that evening was a sign of his respect and trust in our new friendship with them.

When she learned that Mark and I would likely serve as teachers one day, Elsie reflected upon her experience of that vocation. She absolutely loved teaching, and she shared how it hurt her to know that some kids she taught had such awful home situations and personal problems. Knowing the complexities of the lives of many of her students, she didn't appreciate how some people romanticized the past, especially with regard to young people. She found it dismissive of the real struggles those young people faced; such an attitude became a strategy to avoid dealing with real-life problems. Those "good old days," said Elsie, contained the seeds of today's challenges. Her diagnosis was that "people don't talk about things, and if you don't talk about something, it won't get better."

She was sharing these insights while clearing the table—a difficult task given her blindness. When we tried to help, she refused, and then Clarence stood and helped guide her into the kitchen even as she constantly bumped into things while moving about the dining room and kitchen. They stopped and turned to us, and Clarence remarked, "Between her bumping and my shuffling, we make for a good band!" They were both people of strong character and faith, and very funny, too. I loved meeting them. When we were leaving, Elsie handed me $25 to help me along the way—I was so struck by the gift of generosity we experienced through Elsie and Clarence. She also asked that we return to their home before we left North Carolina.

Soon we were driving back to St. Martin's, and Larry turned to us and said that now that we had met Clarence and Elsie, they would be praying specifically for us by name every single day for the rest of their lives because they wanted God to protect us and bless us on our journey. When I look back upon my life, it's clear to me that such moments increased my belief in the power of intercessory prayer.

I called my new friend Heidi at Wake Forest the next morning. Good news. Melissa Harris had returned her call and left a message. Melissa told her that yes, she knew Maya Angelou quite well and, in fact, she worked at her real office in Winston-Salem each day from three to five in the afternoons. She asked that Heidi call her again during that time, so when I spoke to her that morning, Heidi told me to come back to Wake Forest in the afternoon so I could be present when she placed that phone call. If the opportunity arose, I would be able to chat with Melissa directly. I realized that Heidi was carving out possibilities for me behind the scenes.

In the afternoon I made my way back to campus and went to the dean's office to greet Heidi. When I arrived, she returned Melissa's call, and they chatted for a bit, Heidi telling her about my reason for coming to Wake Forest. She then handed the phone to me, and I spoke directly with Melissa, who listened attentively and came across as kind. She said that she would bring my situation to the attention of Maya Angelou's personal secretary and then call right back.

I waited in the office for a short time when Heidi came out to say that Melissa was back on the telephone. Melissa told me that I should bring the letters I had sent to the office where she was currently working for Maya Angelou; she provided the street address and a description of the building. I should bring the letters right away, and she said she would personally deliver them to Maya Angelou. Things were starting to move in a good direction!

I thanked Heidi and then ran to the office building, which was a bit of a hike from Wake Forest. I got to the unmarked house just before five o'clock, and when I walked in, it was obvious that I had entered a pretty important space. On the walls were all sorts of framed honorary degrees, poems, and photos. Stacks of mail were visible in a side room, and I thought of how likely it was that my letters were buried somewhere in the midst of those piles. It was delightful simply to be in that office space.

I didn't see Melissa—to this day, I haven't met her—but the secretary knew exactly who I was and why I was there. She took my letters and said that she'd give them to Melissa (I had kept copies of the ones I had sent earlier). Then I gave her the phone number to St. Benedict and told her I could be reached there. I thanked her and then left the office filled with hope. I had done everything I could to facilitate some sort of encounter.

I remained back at St. Martin where I waited for the call, and my waiting continued until Saturday, when, filled with growing discouragement and impatience, I decided to call Melissa. I had been quite hesitant to do so because it was nearing the end of the semester; the last thing I wanted to do was harass a student who already had plenty to attend to with intense final exams and a looming graduation. However, staring at the phone at the parish for those days was beginning to depress me.

Melissa told me that she had personally given the letters to Maya Angelou that Thursday at 5:15, along with the phone number for the parish. But Dr. Angelou was leaving North Carolina that evening for some speaking engagements. If I hadn't yet heard from her, it was unlikely that I would. Melissa explained that Maya Angelou was so heavily scheduled, she probably just didn't have the time or opportunity to contact me. I thanked Melissa for her kind help.

I suppose I was glad at least to know that my waiting had ended, but I was pretty disappointed. All that distance traveled and all that effort exerted, yet nothing to show for it. I felt rejected, which sounds childish, but at that time in my life this experience had become so closely linked to my fragile idealism.

In some ways I felt that I had failed as a pilgrim. The journey was unusual to begin with because the destination was a person, not a place. Now it seemed that the person didn't have any desire to be known by me. The disappointment I felt was magnified because until that point, so much seemed to have been working in my favor. But here I was, empty-handed, seemingly because of my naïveté.

Quickly I grew tired of feeling sorry for myself and began to reconsider my self-pity as I recalled the many people who had helped me along the way, especially the kind women I had met at Wake Forest. I remembered Fr. Larry Hunt and the new friends made at St. Benedict Parish. I had never met African American Catholics before, and this parish had made us feel so warmly welcome, especially at the daily Mass we attended. Their prayerful petitions inspired me because of their desire to be intercessors on behalf of their loved ones. Each day they offered the same prayers: praising God for another day of life and for the gifts of family and friendship. There was no self-pity—only gratitude.

Through the recollection of the goodness and kindness I had experienced, I soon found within myself a growing heart of gratitude for this time in Winston-Salem. I knew that it was time to leave North Carolina. As we prayerfully conversed about the pilgrimage, Mark and I recognized a desire to head toward Washington, DC. When we told him of our intention to move along, Larry insisted on buying our bus tickets to Washington—a final act of generosity. We would leave at nighttime because it was less expensive to ride through the night. We prepared a dinner for him for our good-bye, and we also made a batch of homemade brownies that we took over to our friends Clarence and Elsie as an expression of our gratitude to them. Larry brought us to the depot, and we said good-bye to this kind Jesuit priest who had so warmly welcomed us into his home and into his Jesuit life for the entire week. I will never forget Fr. Larry Hunt and the kindness he showed us so many times during our stay at St. Martin. Nor would I forget the other friends we had made in Winston-Salem. My disappointment in missing Maya Angelou had been replaced with gratitude, and it was with a lighter heart that I boarded the bus and began the long nighttime journey to the nation's capital.

5

A Capital Surprise

Our Greyhound ride was uneventful, except for the portion between Greensboro, North Carolina, and Richmond, Virginia. For some reason, the bus driver took on more people than the bus could hold. It was the middle of the night, and people were sitting on the floor in the aisle, and some were standing. It meant for a long night's journey with little opportunity to sleep.

When Mark and I arrived in Washington, DC, it was early Sunday morning. We were at Union Station, which is quite close to the capitol. Mark knew from a college semester in Washington that there was a Jesuit Catholic parish nearby, so we decided to wait outside the station for some time to pass before we headed toward Saint Aloysius Gonzaga Church. We hoped to stay with the Jesuit community there. There was a Jesuit high school there as well, so we imagined there would be a substantial Jesuit community and therefore a greater likelihood that we could stay with them.

The church was nearly empty when we arrived, except for the priest who was preparing for Mass. He saw us and walked up to greet us. We were quite early for the service, and I'm sure he was curious to find out about these two young men with backpacks; we were also quite unkempt from a night of travel. When we told him we were Jesuit novices on pilgrimage, he first insisted that we follow him into the community where we would leave our bags because he didn't want us to be burdened with them during the Mass. "You'll stay with us," he said, and I was happy to receive this instant invitation. We returned as Mass was beginning in the lower church space, for the upper church was being restored. Saint Aloysius is a magnificent place, a must-see when visiting Washington.

When the service was concluding, the priest requested visitors to introduce themselves to the congregation. Well, I really didn't want to call attention to myself; I was sure I looked exactly like how I felt after having been awake on a bus for most of the night. When we didn't respond, the priest singled us out, asking the Jesuit novices to stand in order to be recognized. We stood up and said hello to the parishioners, who gave us a rousing round of applause. Then came the closing song.

As we were leaving our seats after the dismissal, two women who were sitting behind us stopped and asked us about the Jesuits. We explained to them that the Jesuits are an order of religious men in the Catholic Church, and that we were novices who were at the beginning of the training to become Jesuit priests. They introduced themselves as Janae and Melissa.

After this brief exchange, the two of us wanted to make ourselves useful, so we started to collect books from the church pews. As we were putting them back into the shelves, these same two women approached us again. This time they were with two people with disabilities, Mike and Eileen, who had been singing in the choir.

Janae and Melissa explained to us that they were assistants in the L'Arche community in Washington and that Mike and Eileen were core members of the community. They wanted to know if we would like to join them at their house for lunch.

Well, this was an uncanny coincidence and the source of an instant, warm friendship *and* a delightful reunion, for both of us had recently served in L'Arche communities in different places and had such affection for our experiences in that ministry. I remember wondering if this was mere coincidence or the hand of God at work.

While we were eating our lunches there, we told stories about our shared experiences of and love for L'Arche and how much we loved being a part of such a beautiful and loving movement. We talked about Jean Vanier, Henri Nouwen, and Sister Sue Mosteller. I told Melissa and Janae about the friends I had made in Toronto. We had been in those other L'Arche communities only a month earlier, so this encounter at the church in Washington was a great delight, because the prior experiences were so fresh in our memories.

They asked what brought us to Washington. I explained that we novices underwent various experiments during our training and that our time at L'Arche was one of them. I told them that now we were in the midst of the pilgrimage experiment and that this was why we were in Washington.

They were interested in knowing where our journey had taken us thus far. I explained that I had been in pursuit of the poet Maya Angelou and that Mark and I had just arrived in Washington that morning, having come from Winston-Salem, North Carolina. I told them about my efforts to meet her and how I had failed. I told Melissa that a student at Wake Forest who shared her name had been immensely helpful to me along the way and that I found it interesting that God had brought another Melissa into the pilgrimage.

When I finished explaining what had happened at Wake Forest, our table of new friends became quiet. Melissa looked directly at me with determined focus and then began to smile brightly. She explained that later in the week she was going to attend a conference in New York City. Maya Angelou was the keynote speaker. She paused and then asked, "Would you like to join me?"

My heart leaped, yet I felt a strange contradiction. It was quite obvious that what was occurring was no mere coincidence. I could sense a growing excitement with what was unfolding before me; somehow the hand of God was at work in all these introductions and the timing of everything that had happened on this pilgrimage. But I also felt a kind of stubbornness and anxiety because I had no control over what was happening. Why would I go down to New York City, the largest city in the nation, after having spent so much of the pilgrim journey in pursuit of this elusive human being? It seemed neither practical nor wise—I had already tried so hard to meet her, and only a short time earlier I had resolved that it was time to move on. I think I felt a need to salvage somehow what had felt like a failed pilgrimage.

Melissa said she would be happy to have me join her when she drove to New York on Thursday. Besides, it was only Sunday, and I hadn't any idea how long I would stay in Washington. Suddenly I heard myself telling Melissa that I didn't think joining her in New York was realistic. Nor did I want to risk losing more time chasing such an elusive dream.

We were finished with lunch, and Mark and I knew that we needed to get back to the Jesuit community. We hadn't really met those Jesuits yet, and if we were going to stay with them, it was important to be properly introduced. Plus, neither of us had bathed, and I felt exhausted from being on the bus all night.

As we were leaving, Melissa handed me a quickly scribbled note. It contained the name of the conference she was attending in New York City where Maya Angelou was speaking and the toll-free phone number for the conference sponsor, the Omega Institute. She included her phone number, too, and said that if I should change my mind, I should let her know.

Janae drove us back to the church, and from there we headed to the Jesuit community. During our time with the Jesuits at Gonzaga, they treated us with tremendous kindness. I learned quickly that the Jesuits of that part of the United States, what is called the Maryland Province, are thoughtful gentlemen and gracious hosts. When we sat for dinner that evening, the community's entire attention was upon us. They wanted to know all about our pilgrimage thus far. What followed was a lively discussion about young people and the important decisions they have to make. If you get to know Jesuits (and I hope you do), you'll discover that because they most often work in the world of education, they have great insight into the lives of the young. The Jesuits of Gonzaga High School were no exception. What I most recall from that table conversation was their gratitude for the generosity of and cooperation with their students. They also expressed concern about the lack of guidance and discernment that the young had in their own lives and the added pressure these deficits placed upon the school and the important formation it offered.

When dinner was finished, Mark and I strolled around the National Mall. It was freezing outside—and I hadn't brought any warm clothing for the journey. Wrongly, I assumed that May 1 in Washington would be warm. Mark wanted to visit Georgetown, our Jesuit university, to see if their Jesuit community library had a book he wanted to consult. We showed up at the Georgetown Jesuit community unannounced and once again were welcomed graciously by the Jesuits gathered in the living room that evening. We chatted with them for a while and then made our way back to Gonzaga. The first thing I did was hit the shower because I was so cold from walking out in the chilly weather, and I was still exhausted from the long night of travel.

The next day I went down to the newly opened Holocaust Museum. If you have been to Washington, you know that besides the stunning monuments located throughout the National Mall, there are tremendous museums to visit for free. At that time the Holocaust Museum was *the* museum to see in Washington; it was receiving rave reviews for its sophistication in presenting such a complex and tragic past. We went because one of the Jesuits recommended it to us, but we needed to get tickets early because of the crowds. We got our tickets, but our admission time was later, so we returned to Gonzaga and spent the rest of the morning and afternoon working at the McKenna Center at the parish. We packed bags and bags of food for the homeless.

We returned to the Holocaust Museum in the afternoon and spent about four hours there. It was a brilliantly designed exhibit, the first museum I'd ever visited that incorporated so much historical video footage. I learned much, and it left me feeling sad and confused. How could humanity be so cruel? There were three Jewish paratroopers who had entered Hungary and were caught. One was named Hannah Senesh, who was almost twenty-three (my age at the time) and a poet. Her words especially made a lasting impression on me. The Nazis captured her, but she refused to reveal any information to them. They executed her. She left behind these lines, which I put to memory then and there:

> Blessed is the match consumed
> in kindling flame
> Blessed is the flame that burns
> in the secret fastness of the heart
> Blessed is the heart with strength to stop
> its beating for honor's sake
> Blessed is the match consumed
> in kindling flame.

What most impressed me was the final section of the museum—videos of Holocaust survivors providing testimony of their experience. They spoke of faith, torture, love, and death.

I sat down and couldn't really describe what I was feeling. Was I tired? excited? perplexed? What should I be doing on this pilgrimage? Here I was in Washington, DC, twenty-three years old, and I didn't know what I was doing. I was all over the place because I had lost my focus and purpose on the journey—at least that's how it seemed.

Maybe I should go down to the Children's Defense Fund and see if I could work there? I had just read a great little book by the founder, Marian Wright Edelman, and I thought that making some connection with that organization might bring me a greater sense of purpose. Then I thought that maybe I should leave and head toward New York City. What to do? Where to go? And for what purpose?

The next day, Tuesday, I wandered around Washington, trying to find someplace where I might be helpful. I began at the Children's Defense Fund and spoke with someone who told me that Edelman was out of town for two weeks. I was directed then to the mayor's youth initiatives office, who sent me to the Children's Trust Neighborhood Initiative, who set up a meeting for me that Friday.

It was crazy. I felt empty-handed, vulnerable, and purposeless, and I was setting up a real goose chase for myself. What I most hoped for from the pilgrimage had not happened, and now that I had some distance from my efforts, I wasn't even sure about what I had been trying so hard to accomplish in the first place.

I walked a great deal that day, trying to find those offices and just trying to think about life. My mind raced. I questioned my pilgrimage—was I doing the best I could? Was I challenging myself to reach a higher potential? Was my staying with Jesuits making things too easy? What about having a companion? I loved Mark and enjoyed working with him, yet I wondered whether I was relying on my friend too much. As I passed a phone booth, I reached into my pocket and found the note Melissa had written to me earlier. I decided to call the Omega Institute, the organization that was having the conference in New York. From that brief phone conversation I learned that I could attend by registering for one day at a cost of $105. I didn't have that kind of money. Plus I didn't know New York City and was afraid of going there alone. I hung up the phone, took out my journal, and looked up the phone number for Maya Angelou's office in North Carolina. I wondered if that office could get the conference fee waved for me. The answer was quick: no.

As I stood by that phone booth, it seemed so clear that everything was indicating a dead end. I could see this rationally but could not stop wondering about whether I should go to New York. After all, maybe I had learned that Maya Angelou was going to be in New York because I was *supposed* to know that. Maybe God was trying to tell me something.

I returned to Gonzaga grumpy and completely drained of any remaining confidence in myself. I felt completely fragile. We sat at dinner with two Jesuits, the superior of the house, Fr. Henry Hasking, and Fr. Joe Lingan, the house minister who served as campus minister at the high school. Having these dinner companions proved to be a game changer for me. We felt an instant connection to Fr. Henry and Fr. Joe. It turned out that Henry was a Jesuit classmate of our friend from Winston-Salem, Father Larry Hunt. These two Jesuits offered nothing other than great confidence and encouragement. Henry shared with us that he had revived the novice pilgrimage in the Maryland Province back when he was the novice master a few years earlier. He said that for him, the whole point of the pilgrimage was to cultivate complete confidence in and dependence on God. He discovered that among his novices the real challenge they faced was learning how to beg. Worldly pride and stubborn self-dependence had to be overcome for the graces of pilgrimage to emerge. The ultimate purpose of each particular pilgrimage was shrouded in mystery. Henry then turned directly to me, looked straight into my eyes, and said, "The purpose of your pilgrimage might not be known until months from now. If you knew the reasons now, well, you wouldn't have any need for trust. The truth is that you're being led in freedom all the time. I can't make you believe that, but I believe it. You're right where you are supposed to be as a pilgrim."

I needed to hear that. I sensed that Henry was utterly trustworthy, and I knew right then that whatever he would tell me was spoken because of its value for the remainder of the pilgrimage. I remained silent, hoping he would continue talking. I think Henry sensed this in me, for a moment later he offered a little teaching on how to beg. I found it quite surprising, because I hadn't disclosed the discomfort I had been experiencing in Washington. I would soon discover that the strategy he described would bear great fruit. It had been relatively easy to beg on the Appalachian Trail because at those nighttime shelters I was placed into relationships almost automatically. Then at Wake Forest, I found myself surrounded both by peers and thoughtful people who, because they worked with students, were especially tuned in to what I might need. In Washington, I think I felt uncomfortable at the subway stops and on the streets because I was a complete stranger. I was self-conscious and uncertain how to relate because the structures for relating I had relied on in the earlier situations were now absent. All I had was who I was, and part of me felt that it wasn't good enough.

Well, Henry told me to consider the situation from the perspective of the person I was approaching. By this he meant that rather than explain in detail my situation to a person with the hope of some sort of response (telling a "sob story" as Henry called it), I should try being very direct. If I saw someone on the subway eating a big pretzel, I should go up to her and tell her that I'm hungry and would she please give me half of that pretzel. Henry observed that people often have more than they need, and if asked directly, they will be generous in sharing what they have, especially if what is requested is right in front of them, in their hands. "You need courage to ask for what you need in life, and that starts by believing that you are worthy of what it is that you seek. If you weren't, then you wouldn't even think of asking for it. Everything is here to help you on the journey. That's by God's design and plan. Who knows—maybe if you get good at this as a pilgrim, you might start doing it in your prayer, too!"

Joe was also very kind during that dinner. He told Mark and me that it was a delight for their Jesuit community to have us among them. He even said he was proud of us for being so brave on our pilgrimage. He observed that it wasn't easy to come to a place where one is unknown by others and then to take the risk of being known and knowing others. "That's a spiritual gift that God is cultivating in your young Jesuit life, and it is a gift that will unfold into the future if you let it." He became reflective. "Jesuit pilgrims enter all sorts of doors in life. A Jesuit meets people right where they are, and then through God's grace, perhaps he can help bring them through the door of his own heart and mind and lead them to a deeper encounter with God. Here at Gonzaga, you've been doing this, and you've been doing it well."

These observations meant a great deal to me, especially because I felt that I had been doing the exact opposite. The example of kindness expressed by Jesuits such as Henry and Joe reminded me how easily I respond to encouragement. Such reassurance goes a long way, and I knew that my attitude had shifted completely during the course of that meal. I left the table feeling absolutely energized and with a newfound hope. That night as I went to bed, I asked God to help me discern where I should go as a pilgrim. I asked him to help me be happy in this present moment of life—I was in good company—and to help me stay open to his will for whatever came next.

The next day I woke up with the beginning of what would soon become an awful cold. Though I felt quite sick, I wanted to be attentive to the day because there were important decisions I needed to make. Mark and I began to discuss the remainder of our shared experiment. We agreed that the time had come for us to separate, but we recognized, too, that our doing so would involve a higher level of discomfort. One of the gifts of the pilgrimage was learning how to work and live with another Jesuit. We played well off each other, and I believe that part of that gift was growing in the art of conversation. We had a lot of time to talk about important matters, and that influenced the way we interacted with others. Everywhere we went we became more confident in explaining who we were and what we were doing and in learning about the people we encountered. Pilgrimage had become a team effort, one upon which I relied a great deal. Our separation meant that the next step of the pilgrimage would involve greater vulnerability and insecurity and, therefore, more dependence on God. From the earlier conversation with Joe and Henry, I knew this was right, even though the thought of it caused anxiety.

As I pondered the change we were about to make, I could sense that God was inviting me to go to New York. I had been reflecting upon my time in Washington. It started with such a surprise—meeting Melissa from L'Arche and her sharing with me the information about that lecture in New York. This was followed by an extended battle with deep insecurity. I took the risk of revealing my fears and anxieties. The fruit of doing so was an outpouring of encouragement that placed me at an important crossroad. A mysterious door into the near future had opened, and I could enter it or walk away from it in freedom. When I thought about the week's events in their entirety, it seemed that they suggested a significant convergence of realities, which pointed me to New York City.

I sat quietly with this possibility and pondered it. On Thursday this direction was confirmed when I went to the Basilica of the National Shrine of the Immaculate Conception, the grand Catholic shrine on the campus of the Catholic University of America. Two gifts were revealed in that great church. First, my heart was moved by a side altar for Mary, Queen of Ireland. It was the prayer inscribed upon the wall that struck me with reassurance.

> Jesus
> with me
> before me
> behind me
> on my right
> on my left

I knew that if the Lord was with me, all around me, I would be protected. All would be well. In the words of Maya Angelou, "*I knew that if God loved me, then I could do wonderful things, I could try great things, learn anything, achieve anything.*"

I paused to record this prayer in my journal, and then as I continued to wander the basilica, I was surprised to come across another side altar dedicated to six Jesuit saints: Ignatius Loyola, Francis Xavier, Stanislaus Kostka, Alphonsus Rodriguez, John Berchmans, and Aloysius Gonzaga.

St. Stanislaus is the patron saint of Jesuit novices, and this statue depicts him with pilgrim's staff and satchel. Encountering St. Stanislaus as a pilgrim gave me great consolation because it confirmed that I was called to continue the journey. I knelt in front of this side altar and asked for the prayerful intercession of these exemplar Jesuits. I prayed for guidance and wisdom. With the eyes of my heart I saw each of these saints come before me and place his hand upon my head as he prayed over me. From St. Stanislaus I asked for special intercession; perhaps he could provide me some sense of interior confirmation. I needed greater courage for what was next in my life as a pilgrim, for I still felt a lingering fear of the unknown. The difference now was that there was simultaneously a burning confidence in where I stood and where I was headed.

After I left the National Basilica, Mark and I went to the Capitol building to see the two Jesuits represented in Statuary Hall, Eusebio Kino and Jacques Marquette. When we approached the building, we noticed a demonstration on the steps. It was a protest against the School of the Americas, a United States-sponsored school located in Georgia where some Central and South American soldiers were trained. The demonstration was for the Jesuits and their two companions who were killed in El Salvador; their murderers had been trained at that facility. These protestors were on day 25 of a 40-day hunger strike. We were introduced to a Maryknoll Catholic priest named Roy Bourgeois, who told us they were striking in order to call attention to a congressional bill that he hoped would lead to the closing of that military training facility.

When he learned that we were Jesuit pilgrims, Fr. Bourgeois paused and said he wanted to introduce us to a Jesuit who was with him. Who would have thought we would run into a Jesuit protesting on the front steps of the United States Capitol? This priest, Bill Bichsel, was from Tacoma, Washington. He told us to call him "Bix." He too was engaged in the hunger strike. At first glance, you would have thought he was homeless. We learned that he did, in fact, live among the homeless at the Catholic Worker House in Washington. Bix was a delightful character to chat with. When he found out we were in the midst of pilgrimage, he shared with us a story of his own journey of six months, hitchhiking around the United States, wandering and letting himself be moved wherever the Spirit invited him to go. He encouraged us about our pilgrimage, telling us that the Holy Spirit was guiding us and to trust that the Spirit was at work.

He said to me, "The best is still to come. You better get moving." That was exactly what I wanted to hear from the convergence of all these important conversations with Jesuits in Washington. I felt a surge of energy, and I decided right then on those steps that I would go to New York City.

6

The Kind Marquis

The next day, Mark and I ate lunch at Gonzaga High School, and then I hurried off to get to the bus depot so that I could catch the Greyhound for the long ride up to New York City. Unfortunately, the cold virus that had begun its work the day before was now a full-blown mess in my head, and as I settled into the bus seat, the hum and movement of the vehicle quickly lulled me to sleep. I awoke in a groggy haze as we neared the city. I was disoriented by the density and rush of the surroundings outside the comfort of my window. In my congested and foggy mind I sensed a growing panic because of an expanding doubt about the wisdom of my coming to New York by myself. It was evening, and the approaching darkness seemed to confirm my growing dread as we arrived at the terminal. I didn't know what I was doing.

I exited the bus and hovered around the station, trying to muster up the courage to go out and walk, but I didn't know where to go. I started to wander around the Port Authority neighborhood, simply trying to get a sense of my surroundings. While I was still near the station, I talked to a young woman who told me that a group of hotels was not far, so I started walking toward the area she described. Sensing a need for more specific confirmation, I began to approach passersby, asking them to point me in the direction of the Marriott

Marquis, the hotel that was hosting the Omega Institute's conference. I engaged a young man sitting on the front steps of a large
building, and I learned from him that I had been wandering in the
wrong direction. To my surprise he stood up and escorted me down
Eighth Avenue and then West 46th Street toward the hotel. I think
he could sense that I hadn't a clue where I was or what I was doing.
As we walked, we began to chat. He told me to call him "Jersey"; he
appeared to be maybe a year older than me. Perhaps it was because
we were roughly the same age that we connected so easily—there was
a curious familiarity and gentleness that I felt with him. He revealed
that he was homeless and addicted to drugs. After walking some distance, we were near enough to the hotel that he could point it out
to me in the skyline. Knowing that I was in the right area gave me
some reassurance that I would be okay, and I suggested that we sit
again for a moment because we were still talking. Besides, I noticed
that his shoes were in shreds, and I regretted that he had walked such
a distance on my behalf.

I was wearing the hiking boots I used on the Appalachian Trail,
and I also had an old pair of sneakers in my backpack, so I asked him
if he would like to have my boots. He did and we sat down on some
steps for the exchange. While we were sitting together, he asked me
if I was staying at the hotel. I told him that I wasn't but that I had
hoped to attend a talk there in the morning. He asked me where I
was going to stay for the night, and I said I had no idea. He told me
to be very careful and not to talk to strangers, except for right at that
moment. We had a good laugh, and he walked away in my boots.

A short while later I was in front of that grand hotel. I sat down
and began to develop a strategy for surviving in New York City
through the night and into the next day. The whole thing seemed
very complicated to me now that I was in the city and could see the
building. I think I was perplexed mostly because I didn't have a place

to sleep that night, nor did I have the money to register for the conference the next morning. I couldn't think of any good ideas, so I continued to remain seated outside the hotel. I became aware of the hotel's vigilant porters and security men. I could tell that loitering around the Marriott Marquis would cause suspicion and then complicate my ability to enter the conference the next day, so it seemed wise to create some distance between the hotel and me, at least for the night. I decided that my plan would be to walk continuously through the night around that part of the city and then return to the hotel early in the morning to sneak into the conference hall before the regular attendees arrived. I wouldn't wander too far and risk getting lost. It wasn't a very creative plan, but I couldn't think of anything better. I figured that continuous walking was the best I could do for the time being.

So I began to walk in New York City, and it quickly became apparent that I was no longer on the Appalachian Trail, nor was I at Wake Forest University. Everything around me was moving, and I felt overwhelmed and small in the midst of both the rush of people and the towering skyscrapers. On the sidewalk I ran into the actor Ethan Hawke, or at least I'm pretty sure it was him. He was in a movie I'd seen months earlier in Toronto called *Reality Bites*. For some odd reason I decided to approach him to ask if his reality still bit. He looked at me blankly, shrugged, and kept walking.

I was wandering aimlessly on either Sixth or Seventh Avenue and not feeling well because of my cold. I figured that since I had slept for a short time on the bus, I would be able to sustain well enough through the night. This seemed to be, truly, my only real option, but as I strolled, I realized that this idea of walking around the city wasn't the best. I had to remind myself that I was a pilgrim and that the path had led me to New York City. God would provide; recalling this in the midst of my uncertainty gave me a bit of hope.

After a while I came across a building that had an entrance labeled "Saint Francis Xavier." I recognized this familiar name; Xavier was a Spanish Jesuit known both for his zealous missionary work and for being the closest of Ignatius's companions when the Society of Jesus was founded. Upon seeing his name, I stopped abruptly, approached the door, and pressed against it. To my surprise, it was unlocked—remarkable given that this was New York City and it was nighttime. I sensed God's providence at work. I knew in that moment that all would be well.

I stepped inside, and two men and a woman were walking toward me in the entranceway. They said they were just about to lock the door to the building, which was a church or a social hall. They must have sensed that I was lost or afraid; they introduced themselves, I think to put me at ease. Having just emerged from the hustle of the city, I was dumbfounded by the stillness of that hallway and then the surprise of learning who they were. I was also struck by their gentleness with me—a complete stranger—as they introduced themselves as *Jesuits* and a Catholic nun: Michael Donahue, John Bucki, and Sister Honora. They asked me who I was and if I needed their help. When I told them I was a Jesuit pilgrim novice, it was their turn to look surprised.

Sister Honora smiled and looked at the two Jesuits standing with her. She asked me, "Where are you going tonight?" I explained that I had just arrived in the city by bus and that I was planning on wandering the streets through the night. I had only stumbled across this place and stopped for a moment because of Francis Xavier's name. I didn't mean to bother them. I would keep going.

Sister Honora sharply shook her head and said something to the effect of "Absolutely not. Come, Pilgrim." They insisted I stay with them—they were concerned about my plan for the night. Together we exited that building and walked to a small Jesuit residence nearby on West 17th Street.

Truthfully, I was relieved and delighted. My cold was irksome, and the bus ride had worn me out. I was also overwhelmed by the city itself. And I hadn't a clue where I would go for the rest of the night. I perceived this particular moment to be holy, a number of convergences taking place that reassured me. Even while the events unfolded, I sensed God's purpose and providence. All I needed to do, which was also the most important thing, was simply to receive what God was revealing.

In this little religious community in the heart of Manhattan I had a tiny room to stay in. These new friends could sense that I needed rest and quiet, so they got me settled and then left me for the night. That I would have any shelter whatsoever was the furthest thing from my mind in terms of possible outcomes for the night in that gigantic, bustling city. There was a futon in the room, and I still had my blanket from the Appalachian Trail. Only a short time earlier I had been fearful and tense, but as I lay in that little room, I found myself peaceful and assured.

Being safe at Francis Xavier afforded me the opportunity to formulate a new plan, which was to doze a bit but not fall asleep. Lacking a watch or alarm, I knew that with my cold, if I fell asleep I might oversleep and fail to accomplish my one goal for my having come to New York. Plus, I felt content just resting in the joy of what had transpired. My new vision was to leave Francis Xavier early at sunrise and walk back to the hotel well before the conference convened. I would sneak into the keynote address that Maya Angelou was scheduled to deliver.

So there I sat upon the futon, wrapped in a blanket in a sort of prayerful vigil. A few hours later I rose with the sun. Equipped with my backpack, I headed toward the Marriott Marquis. Maya

Angelou would be speaking at the hotel at 8:45 a.m.; leaving around six o'clock would give me ample time to get into the conference without being noticed. I arrived at the hotel and inquired about the conference location. The concierge noted that I was quite early. I told him that I didn't mind waiting, so he directed me to the ballrooms. When I stepped off the escalator, I realized I hadn't arrived early enough, for there were people setting up the conference registration tables right in front of the ballroom entrances I had hoped to bypass undetected. I hadn't bathed that morning as I had risen so early and didn't want to disturb the others who were sleeping in that small Jesuit community. My dirty backpack didn't help either, and I wasn't properly dressed for a special conference in a nice hotel.

So I decided to pretend to be very interested in the details of the ballroom lobby, hoping that I would blend undetected into the developing activity that surrounded me. I walked nonchalantly toward the ballroom entrance only to be called out by a woman who was now eyeing me as she sat at the registration table. She seemed to be the keeper of the gate, and I am certain that I looked sketchy. She asked if she could help me find something.

I didn't have time to think of anything clever so I told her exactly what I was about to do: attend the 8:45 Maya Angelou lecture that was sponsored by the Omega Institute. This woman worked for the Omega Institute, and she asked where my conference registration badge was. I told her I didn't have one but that I wasn't there for the conference at all—I only desired to hear the keynote speaker.

Well, she found that rather amusing. She wondered what made me think I could go to a conference talk without attending the conference. She explained how at that very table I could register for the day and then I could go to the talk. I told her that I couldn't register because I didn't have the money—and for some reason that I still don't understand, I added that I didn't even know what the Omega

Institute was or why they were having a conference. This did not impress her. She said that without registration I wouldn't be admitted to the talk.

My situation had suddenly become complicated. In those early morning hours I was not communicating well and had already doomed my plan. In a sort of last-ditch effort I told her it was very important for me to attend the talk, for I had been on the road for weeks, trying to track down Maya Angelou. I'm afraid this little addendum had the unintended effect of making me appear dangerous, as if I were some sort of stalker roaming the United States on the hunt for the poet. The woman was looking at me with even greater perplexity and annoyance. I was unshaven, and because of my cold, my nose was dry and crusted and my voice was hoarse. I had a smelly backpack because of my sweaty sojourn upon the Appalachian Trail. I was in sneakers, and my clothing was dirty. I can only imagine what was going through her head.

She kept staring at me and then I said, "Please. Would you let me attend this presentation?" She told me that it wouldn't be fair—others had paid to attend the conference. I didn't know what else I could say to build my case. Mine was fundamentally an appeal for kindness. However, I had messed things up in such a short time that any further effort would surely feel hollow.

At that moment other people, maybe conference attendees, began to gather within the ballroom lobby. I didn't want to call attention to my awkward situation. A coworker came to the table to help check badges, and I began to plead my case with her. The first worker announced to her colleague that only paid registrants could enter the ballroom. I piped in somewhat desperately, "Please let me in. I've come all the way from Minnesota." The first told the second, "He doesn't even know what the Omega Institute is."

The coworker asked me, "How did you find out about this conference?"

"A girl named Melissa told me."

"Who is Melissa?"

I told her that I'd met Melissa at church and that she was probably at the conference.

"Did she come from Minnesota, too?"

"No, I met her at church in Washington." I listened to myself and realized that I sounded absolutely bizarre. Rather than go into more of the strange details, I decided to ask again: Would they simply please make an exception and let me in? They were adamant that they would not. Right then a third person came to the table. Her name was Andrea Johnson, and she seemed to be an official with the organization. The other two had reached their limit in dealing with me, and Andrea must have seen that there was a problem brewing at the registration table. She asked me what was going on.

This was my final chance to make my case, so I took a deep breath, looked her in the eye, and tried to keep it simple: I was a Jesuit who had been on the road for weeks trying to meet Maya Angelou. Through the most unusual of circumstances I had learned she was speaking at this conference and, though I couldn't afford the registration fee, I would appreciate it if she would consider allowing me to attend the morning lecture. She stood there for a moment and looked at me. I could tell that she was a gentle person. I don't know what was going on in her mind, but she paused and then looked me right in the eye and said, "You promise me that you'll attend only this lecture and then leave immediately afterward?" I said, "Absolutely!" She said, "Make him a badge and let him in," and then to me, "As soon as Maya Angelou is done speaking you must come here and turn in your badge." Her colleagues were incensed.

I was in!

I walked into the ballroom and saw hundreds and hundreds of chairs arranged in orderly rows for the presentation. It was still quite early, and only a handful of people were in the room. I walked to the front row of chairs, dropped my backpack on the floor, and sat down just to the left of the podium. I figured that it was okay to get a good seat.

Gradually, the room filled with people, the volume of their voices growing intense. At 8:45, a sudden hush came over the room while Maya Angelou emerged from a side entrance and approached the podium. The room exploded with applause. A smile lit up her face.

Maya Angelou's presentation explored the depth of human communion, which is always in existence, even in the midst of humanity's great diversity. She gently reminded us that we are fundamentally more alike than we are unalike.

I would have enjoyed her presentation in any case, but I did now even more so because I had studied her life. I already knew so much of her story, and now I savored being able to listen to that beautiful voice live and in person.

She shared some of her poetry. She referred to her life story. She spoke of the young and her hope in the future they would create. She spoke of the past and the fruit that it could bear for the present.

I knew precisely, the moment she spoke her final words, that it was absolutely for them that God had drawn me to this encounter. I experienced an overwhelming fullness of understanding, realizing that I had been led to that moment and venue to hear Dr. Angelou speak these twenty-six words:

"All my conscious life and energies have been dedicated to the most noble cause: the liberation of the human mind and spirit, beginning with my own."

Upon her conclusion there was thunderous applause, and then she turned to leave the podium. I remained in my seat, stunned and satisfied. I had brought some copies of the letters I had been sending along the way, and before the presentation started I fancied myself approaching her when she concluded and presenting the letters to her. When she finished, however, I had neither the desire nor the need to give them to her. It didn't matter anymore. I just remained seated, pondering and savoring those marvelous final words. I could feel them take root within me. I loved them because they were familiar, a jubilant echo of what our novice master had said to us back in Denver a few months earlier at the beginning of the Spiritual Exercises. "For freedom you have been set free." What Maya Angelou described was what I would gradually come to understand, with precision and clarity, as the center of my vocation as a Jesuit priest. Everything about my training, all my relationships, the many experiences, the gifts of study and prayer and desire—ultimately everything I had received and was yet to receive in life was to be given away, meant for the betterment of others so that they, too, might grow toward the great interior freedom that comes from knowing the profound love of God.

Happily, I remained in New York for seven days. While I spent the nights with the Jesuits, I passed the days moving around the city. From the beginning of my time there I applied the beggar teaching that Henry shared with me earlier in Washington, so while I wandered Central Park, I approached people and asked for half of whatever food was in their hands. Sometimes I was rejected, but I spotted a plethora of bagels and pizza in people's hands and encountered enough generosity to keep me nourished. Henry's wise technique didn't work with soft-serve ice cream cones, however.

Most important, I was growing in the grace of overcoming pride and the accompanying self-consciousness that earlier I had felt when poor and in need. I was learning that sometimes people are in deep need and are profoundly dependent on others. Had the pilgrimage experiment been an exercise of self-dependence and self-sufficiency, I'm sure that I'd still be standing in the streets of Knoxville, Tennessee.

Yet even with that growth I continued to have my struggles. While walking the city on the following Monday, I found myself standing in front of St. Patrick's Cathedral. I entered that beautiful church and spent time in prayer before the noon Mass. Afterward, I left the cathedral and walked toward the United Nations, where I had no success whatsoever begging for food. I was feeling physically weak. I kept walking and out of frustration ended up at St. Patrick's again, where I prayed for a while. It was a place I knew and where I felt safe. Prayer was difficult, though, because I felt so weary. Contributing to the fatigue and discouragement was the volume of noise from visiting tourists. It seemed to escalate by the minute. Feeling rather disheartened, I decided to leave St. Patrick's for a second time. But on my way out I looked to the side and noticed an altar dedicated to Saint Stanislaus Kostka, the Jesuit patron saint of novices. Stanislaus is always depicted with a pilgrim's staff, so encountering him during a desolate moment gave me a burst of encouragement and confidence. After kneeling for some time in prayer at this side altar, I felt compelled to approach an information table at the back of the cathedral. I told the man there that I was hungry, and I asked him if he could help me find something to eat.

The rapid response to my little request still amazes me, for a chain of events unfolded at such speed that my head spun. Seemingly out of nowhere, one lady pressed into my hands a bunch of grapes; another woman whisked me away to the parish house. With each step the surroundings became quieter and quieter. It was as if I were being picked up and carried to safety, and it was happening so quickly that I found it difficult to keep up with her.

Once at the parish house, I was told to sit down at a little dining room table. A short while later an Irish lady named Mary brought me a sandwich. She called for Father Scafidi, and they both sat across the table, watching me while I ate. When I explained who I was and what I was doing, the two of them looked at each other and shook their heads in disapproval. The priest made it absolutely clear that he thought Jesuit novices on pilgrimage an absurd idea. He was concerned about my safety and where I was going.

Then Father Scafidi asked what my parents thought of all this. I told him that they didn't know, for we weren't allowed to call them while we were pilgrims. He looked at Mary, and they both shook their heads with displeasure. Mary said, "The Jesuits. Oh my, oh my." Father Scafidi asked what my parents would think, knowing that I was in New York City, "the largest city in the country, wandering alone and asking people for food, and wandering in St. Patrick's Cathedral, of all places. You Jesuits," he said.

Then he made me give him my parents' phone number, and when I protested, Mary nodded her agreement, so I knew I wasn't going to win that battle. He promptly called and my mom answered. Father Scafidi introduced himself and told my mom that I was eating a sandwich at St. Patrick's Cathedral in New York City and that I was doing fine but that he thought the whole thing was crazy and wanted to make sure that she knew I was doing well.

To this day my mom loves Father Bill Scafidi, though she has never met him.

After the phone conversation, Father Scafidi and Mary continued to sit there and look at me. What were they going to do with this twenty-three-year-old Jesuit? Finally, he broke the silence by asking me what I was going to do next. I said I wasn't certain but I would probably continue to walk around New York City and see what would happen next. He was unimpressed.

He said he had something for me, and then he left the kitchen for a short time. While he was gone, Mary continued to sit with me. "Casey. That's a very good name," she said. "You're Irish." I told her that my mom was Irish and that my dad was French. "God bless your mom," she said.

When he returned a short while later, Father Scafidi reported that he had telephoned a priest named Father Glen, whom he wanted me to meet. Father Glen was one of the founders of a new Catholic community in the Bronx called the Franciscan Friars of the Renewal. Father Scafidi was convinced that I would benefit from meeting him and learning about the friars' growing ministry to the poor. "It's important that while you are here you see what the Spirit is doing for the future. Your generation is starting to make such important contributions. Go and see!"

This kind priest gave me $10 and four subway tokens. He also gave me a small duffel bag and asked that when I no longer needed it to give it to someone in need whom I might meet along the way. As we started to make our way back to the bustling cathedral, Mary slipped me $30 and gave me a big hug and a kiss on the cheek. "That's from your mom."

In the cathedral, Father Scafidi brought me to Our Lady's altar and we knelt in front of a large statue of Mary. First he asked that I pray for his sister, Mary, who had cerebral palsy. She was going to have surgery a few days later. After we both prayed in silence, I started to rise when Father Scafidi placed his hand on my shoulder, signaling that I remain in prayer. Then he offered a prayer on my behalf. As we knelt there in silence, he leaned my way and shared some wisdom that he said would be the most important component of any future ministry for any person I would ever encounter. He turned to me and said,

Be kind.
Be kind.
Be kind!
Remember to be kind to people.
Don't forget to be kind!

He spoke slowly and with much deliberation. That he said this to me repeatedly was at first perplexing, even mildly annoying. I had understood him the first time, so why did he keep saying it?

But the more he repeated it, the more I came to recognize that what he was telling me was simply a clear articulation of what he had been doing earlier. His wise words reflected earlier actions.

I had arrived at that house unannounced and out of nowhere, and I'm certain that both he and Mary had plenty of work to do that afternoon. My arrival was an interruption, yet their reception and warmth made it feel as if they had been expecting me. It was abundantly clear to me that I had been treated with kindness since the moment I stepped inside St. Patrick's Cathedral.

I started to cry then, because I was filled with an absolutely overwhelming sense of how much love, generosity, and *kindness* had been shown to me as a pilgrim during the past weeks. Here I was wandering the country and popping randomly into people's lives, unannounced and needy. Yet I was welcomed, embraced, engaged, encouraged, and loved—no questions asked. I became keenly aware that the Father's hand had been at work.

I recalled the beauty of the Appalachian Trail and how fortunate Mark and I were to have such good weather along our journey. Creation had cared for us and protected us. I thought of the generosity of our fellow hikers who gave me food and, literally, the clothing off their backs. Soon I found myself remembering the students and the staff at Wake Forest University and Larry Hunt and Heidi and Elsie and Clarence, and how much these new friends in North Carolina had gone to such great efforts to support and encourage me, a total stranger.

I considered Melissa at Gonzaga in Washington, DC., and how she invited me to lunch after Mass, Henry's patient instruction and encouragement, and then that thoughtful woman at the Omega Institute in New York City who opened wide the door to the end I had been seeking for so long. I was overcome by the memory of those lovely words that I traveled the nation seeking to receive: *All my conscious life and energies have been dedicated to the most noble cause: the liberation of the human mind and spirit, beginning with my own.*

Suddenly I wanted to do something for God in response to this tremendous generosity. I wanted to give him my very self. In that moment, in that massive cathedral of St. Patrick in New York City, I wanted to give myself away to God. This pilgrimage had shown me my true vocation.

There are many other parts to this pilgrimage story, but they aren't so important. I went from New York to New Orleans, a forty-eight-hour bus ride that began with my sitting next to someone who opened a big bag of aromatic Funyuns and wanted to talk the entire time. In Alabama I watched from my window a large man driving a car next to us on the highway while he chatted away with his passenger in the next seat. His belly rested on the steering wheel, and he kept gesticulating. It was obvious that he was enthusiastic about whatever they were talking about—so much so that he really wasn't paying attention to the road. I watched him turn, literally, into our bus. We had to pull over while the highway patrol came and inspected the bus for damage.

While in New Orleans I slept outside one night in Audubon Park, which was not a good idea. It was unsafe, and I was mistaken for a prostitute several times. One morning I was doing my laundry in the men's restroom of a McDonald's restaurant. I had a sink filled with my socks and underwear, and a worker came in and reprimanded me. I was embarrassed and shouldn't have been doing that, but I had limited options. In New Orleans I met Father Joseph Brown, a Jesuit who taught at Xavier University. He was kind to me and helped me navigate the city. It took a week before I eventually made my way to Chicago, and then to Milwaukee, where I had a great reunion with mentors and friends at Marquette University. From there I returned to Saint Paul, where the journey had begun six weeks earlier.

Back in Minnesota I enjoyed a marvelous reunion with classmates. I knew that pilgrimage had changed me. Physically, I had lost about twenty pounds, so our time was filled with great chats over meals in the novitiate house. Spiritually, I had gained so much. In fact, to this day I maintain that much of what I have needed in life was learned or affirmed on pilgrimage. It remains a subtle reference point for me.

During our debriefing, Father Pat, the novice master, invited us to spend a good amount of time reflecting on what God had done for us through the pilgrim journey. He wanted us especially to ponder how our understanding of simplicity of life was deepened through what we experienced along the way. He also invited us to reflect on our capacity for trust and to notice whether it, too, had deepened.

I knew that the primary gift I had received on pilgrimage was a deeper sense of my vocation, my purpose in life. God used the gift of pilgrimage to teach me the value of freedom, especially inner freedom. It seems to me that a human being often has hunches, or what I would name as movements of the Spirit within the human heart. Without interior freedom, those hunches get dismissed quite easily. I learned on pilgrimage to trust what St. Ignatius received in the Spiritual Exercises and what was later echoed in my own experience of growing as a young Jesuit rooted in those same Exercises:

with interior freedom one can learn to read the movements of the human heart and to grow in the belief of knowing that God is always leading and guiding his beloved daughters and sons. I learned something deeper about freedom—to trust that God both communicates to and leads us gently.

That's what I learned from my Jesuit education—and it is what I continue to learn as a Jesuit. It's what I wanted to share with you.

Afterword: *Verbum Caro Factum Est*

In the Jesuits, when a person finishes the two-year period of living as a novice, he professes vows of poverty, chastity, and obedience. These vows represent the commitment a novice is making to give his life away by entering more fully into the Society of Jesus. With the public profession of these promises there begins the long process of Jesuit intellectual and human formation. The Jesuit novice is no longer called by that name; now he is to be known as a Jesuit *scholastic*.

For me, that training as a scholastic began with an important year of humanities studies at Creighton University, the Jesuit school of Omaha, Nebraska. Just adjacent to that downtown Omaha campus was a small Jesuit community that existed specifically for young Jesuits who were beginning their scholastic training. When I arrived at Creighton, I had an immediate, positive impression of that beautiful little university. I quickly discovered that I loved to study there. The professors were warm and encouraging and the students were friendly and bright. At the heart of the campus stood a beautiful college church, a fountain in front of it. It was an easy place to feel at home.

87

Our course work was strictly rooted in the humanities, which meant that there was ample opportunity to take a variety of academic subjects, with special emphasis on foreign languages. We were encouraged to study music theory and art history, and we even had the time to take art and music lessons. Of course, studies in classical literature figured prominently in our academic program. Our Jesuit superior, Father Gregory Carlson, explained at the beginning of the academic year that the Jesuit plan of studies was designed to build a foundation of Jesuit intellectual life. Ultimately, immersion in the humanities would position us well for the future stages of our intellectual training, which would include years of studies in philosophy and theology. The aim of these courses was to foster in us a deep appreciation for the centuries of contributions made by human beings to the formation of the mind and heart. Encounters with art, music, language, poetry, and literature would enable us to explore more deeply what it meant to be fully human and to celebrate human accomplishments.

In his introductory comments to our community at the beginning of that year, Fr. Carlson asked that we take a moment to reflect on what we imagined it might mean to be fully formed and fulfilled. To help us, he distributed a poem written by the English Jesuit poet Gerard Manley Hopkins and asked that we spend some time studying it.

> As kingfishers catch fire, dragonflies draw flame;
> As tumbled over rim in roundy wells
> Stones ring; like each tucked string tells, each hung bell's
> Bow swung finds tongue to fling out broad its name;
> Each mortal thing does one thing and the same:
> Deals out that being indoors each one dwells;
> Selves—goes itself; *myself* it speaks and spells,
> Crying *What I do is me: for that I came.*

I say more: the just man justices;
Keeps grace: that keeps all his goings graces;
Acts in God's eye what in God's eye he is—
Christ—for Christ plays in ten thousand places,
Lovely in limbs, and lovely in eyes not his
To the Father through the features of men's faces.

It was the poem's beginning that quickly caught my attention. I didn't know what a kingfisher was or what Hopkins meant when he suggested that it could catch fire. But the image piqued my curiosity; I knew I needed to ponder these lines.

I learned that a kingfisher is a bird and that Hopkins's image of its catching fire comes from the fiery red pigment of feathers found under the bird's wings. With careful observation, a person could notice that when a kingfisher begins to take flight, the rapid fluttering of its wings mimics the flickering flames of young fire. Hopkins used this lively image to emphasize the potential of what he believed to be true for all living creatures: every living thing desires to soar—to come to life—so that in rising, all the living "deals out that being indoors each one dwells." It seemed that the poem was accentuating how everything that lives hungers and thirsts for the liberation that comes from the freedom of being fully alive. It was in the personal encounter with the exhilaration flowing from freedom that the voice of the poem cries out with utter confidence and delight: "What I do is me: for that I came."

The kingfisher, it seemed to me, is most fully alive when it ascends majestically in flight. A spirit of fire propels it as it soars joyfully and confidently in freedom through the sky. I soon came to love that poem because of the importance it placed on the human flourishing that comes from liberation.

As I lay in bed that night, my mind continued to be drawn to the heart of the message contained within Hopkins's poem and I began to wonder how the classes we would take during the semester might build upon the truth it introduced. I decided that this piece of literature signaled that the grace of the coming year would be found in courses that emphasized the flourishing of humanity. Soon I began to drift off into sleep with this hopeful prediction for the future.

However, I was startled from sleep's beginnings when another poem entered my mind abruptly. It was a poem I knew from my earlier time in college. Why it surfaced at that time is mysterious to me—perhaps it was because I was once again in an academic environment. Perhaps I remembered it because its imagery was so jarring when I compared it to these new thoughts introduced to my mind through Hopkins. Regardless, I was awakened with a memory from my college freshman English class at Marquette where we had read Paul Laurence Dunbar's "Sympathy." We studied Dunbar's poem in preparation for our unit considering Maya Angelou's autobiography. It was from "Sympathy" that Angelou developed the title of her autobiography, *I Know Why the Caged Bird Sings*.

> I know what the caged bird feels, alas!
> When the sun is bright on the upland slopes;
> When the wind stirs soft through the springing grass,
> And the river flows like a stream of glass;
> When the first bird sings and the first bud opes,
> And the faint perfume from its chalice steals—
> I know what the caged bird feels!
>
> I know why the caged bird beats his wing
> Till its blood is red on the cruel bars;
> For he must fly back to his perch and cling
> When he fain would be on the bough a-swing;
> And a pain still throbs in the old, old scars
> And they pulse again with a keener sting—
> I know why he beats his wing!

I know why the caged bird sings, ah me,
When his wing is bruised and his bosom sore,
When he beats his bars and he would be free;
It is not a carol of joy or glee,
But a prayer that he sends from his heart's deep core,
But a plea, that upward to Heaven he flings—
I know why the caged bird sings!

I could feel a surge of power that emanated from the tension between the words of these two poems. I was so struck by the cruel contrast between the kingfisher's flaming fire, which fueled its rise toward fulfillment, and the hemorrhaging caged bird, the bloodied bars resulting from the futile beating of its trapped wings. The memory of Dunbar's image jolted me, and I sat upright in my bed, my eyes filling with tears as I struggled to hold the opposing words of these two poems together in my heart. I felt despair—the disparity, the gap that existed between the image of these two creatures—it all seemed so unjust.

I paused to catch my breath when my troubled heart was flooded suddenly with a warm and consoling relief. It was with much more subtle and gentle memory that I recalled Maya Angelou and that magnificent description of the beauty contained within *the power of the word*. I remembered how she explained her transformative experience of standing before the reality of God's unconditional divine love. The emerging inner surety that came from knowledge and acceptance of the palpable love of God propelled her upward, as if she were being lifted physically.

The pathway seemed clear. I was reminded of the words of the sixth chapter from the prophet Jeremiah: "Stand by the earliest roads, ask the pathways of old, 'Which is the way to good?' and walk it; thus you will find rest for yourselves." The best way in life was to embrace the unconditional love of God and then live that life with love for God. The bloody caged bird mysteriously transfigures into the fiery, soaring kingfisher. That this was true seemed most apparent to me in Angelou's description of the zeal that comes from tremendous liberation. "I am a big bird winging over high mountains, down into serene valleys. I am ripples of waves on silver seas. I am a spring leaf trembling in anticipation."

That, I reminded myself, is a human being who is being fully human. I lay down and soon was drifting into sleep, the words of Hopkins, Dunbar, and Angelou rising as warm tongues of fire flying above my bed.

The next day brought with it the excitement of a new school year's beginning. Upon completing the first week I reflected on my early impressions of the semester. One course had captured my attention from the very start. A young professor named Brian Hook was teaching "The Hero in Antiquity." This material was almost entirely unknown to me. We would be considering the hero as literary and religious figure and how fate was at work in characters such as Achilles, Aeneas, and Oedipus.

As that semester progressed, I and my classmates labored carefully through the works of Homer, Aeschylus, Sophocles, Aristophanes, Apollonius, and Virgil to consider the ancient attributes of heroism and the evolution and adaptation of the hero down to the present day. The course culminated in a final essay that would allow us to synthesize our thoughts on the qualities of the heroic life. When I began to think about possible topics for the paper, I found myself reflecting upon the life of Maya Angelou. The semester began with my having pondered her words and their relationship to the poems of Dunbar and Hopkins. Those early musings seemed to anchor the semester for me, especially given the year's humanistic focus. For this class, I desired to revisit those early reflections on freedom and then somehow relate them to the qualities of the heroic life we had learned from our reading. It seemed to me that Maya Angelou's was a heroic life; perhaps not in the classical sense but certainly through evolution and adaptation that pointed to these foundational roots. I wanted to explore potential synthesis between these past and present understandings.

In proceeding with my research, I felt compelled to draw from my past pilgrimage experience. This was confirmed in a moment of silent prayer one morning. I felt an inner surety that emerged in the form of an instruction: "Go directly to the source." I needed to think more about what that might mean for my writing—but I had a hunch.

It was October, and the composition wasn't due until early December so I had some time. While I had already decided to write about Maya Angelou as a contemporary hero in American culture, I hadn't yet figured out what that was going to look like or how best to approach it. Maybe I should try again to meet her; this might be the way to "go directly to the source." I decided to ask her for an interview so that we could discuss the topic of the heroic life.

I still had the phone numbers of Maya Angelou's various offices, so I began by phoning her off-campus office in Winston-Salem. I asked the secretary if Maya Angelou was teaching at Wake Forest that semester, and I learned that she was in fact offering two courses: *African and African American Culture* and *African Culture and Impact on U.S. Poetry and Performance.* I hung up the telephone and went to the library because a new resource was available on college campuses that didn't exist when I was a novice, something called the Internet! I used one of Creighton library's new computers and looked up the telephone number for the English department at Wake Forest. With that number in hand, I returned to the Jesuit community and called the department. From the English department I learned that Maya

Angelou was team-teaching the first course with another professor, Dr. Dolly McPherson.

With this new information I returned to the library to use the Internet again, but this time I looked up the phone number for the information desk at Wake Forest. I remembered from my earlier visit that students staffed the information desk, and I had a hunch that having a chance to speak with a student might prove helpful in providing me with some more information about that class. I scribbled this new telephone number into my notes, and then I walked back to the community again and telephoned the Wake Forest desk.

Perhaps it was mere coincidence that the receptionist with whom I had spoken was an undergraduate student enrolled in this team-taught class—but I doubt it. When he revealed this delicious detail, we began to have a rather serious chat. He told me that Angelou and McPherson taught together because they had been friends for many years. I confided in him that I wanted to meet Maya Angelou, and he suggested to me, "Then you should try to come to our class. They're both excellent teachers, and it's a great course!"

After I hung up the phone, I sat at my desk and began to consider all this newly acquired information. I went to my bookshelf and retrieved my pilgrimage journal, for I wanted to find a certain phone number.

The next day I got in touch with my Wake Forest friend Heidi Curtis and asked if she might help me locate a fax number that I could use to try to contact Dolly McPherson directly. I thought that my going through this professor might help me get into the class. I wrote a brief letter to Dr. McPherson, explaining who I was, how I had tried to meet Maya Angelou when I was a Jesuit novice, and the writing project I was undertaking for the course I was taking at Creighton. I told her that I had discovered she was teaching a class with Angelou and that I wondered if she might help me make a connection with her. I finished the letter with: "I know this is a strange request. People often ask me why I have had this desire to meet her—where it comes from. She is such an important person in our human existence, and I appreciate her message. I just think that if somebody is on earth right now that I admire this much, I should do all I can to try to meet her. Thank you for giving this your consideration."

I sent the letter as a fax with some apprehension. An interview was very much a sideline idea for Professor Hook's final composition—I had plenty of material for putting together a good paper, so I knew my topic didn't depend at all upon an interview. By the time I arrived at my room, it seemed that the most important thing that had come from these efforts was that I learned how to go online and how to send a fax—no small matter for 1995!

I fell back into the routine of the semester with my regular course work and the pressures that come from the busy month of November on a college campus. In that Jesuit community we cooked for one another on the weekends. On Sunday it was my turn to prepare dinner. It was early afternoon, and I had already started the meal. I wasn't a good cook by any means, so my strategy back then was to begin my preparations early so that if a disaster arose, I could start over. I was frying bacon to add to the Caesar salad when the phone rang. We had two phone lines for the house, and each room in that community had a phone with an intercom. If someone called the house, one of us would answer and then, after putting the person on hold, we would page the house to find the Jesuit who was being telephoned. I didn't answer it because I was attending to my project on the stovetop. I could see from the blinking light that whoever answered had placed the call on hold. Eventually, the intercom in the kitchen beeped, and a Jesuit announced that I had a phone call.

I turned down the heat and picked up the phone, expecting it to be my parents or one of my siblings.

"Hi, it's Casey."

"Casey, this is Maya Angelou."

"What?"

"This is Dr. Maya Angelou."

"Shut up! Oh my God!"

Yes, indeed. It was Maya Angelou on the phone. Calling me while I was frying bacon. I could tell it was her because of that deep, beautiful voice.

And. I. Said. Shut. Up.

She explained to me that right then she was sitting with her friend Dr. Dolly McPherson and that they together had been reading my faxed letter. "We each have a copy of it in our hands. I would like you to visit my class at Wake Forest next week. Could you come?"

I told her that I needed to get permission but yes, I would be there.

"Good. I'm going to give the phone to Dr. McPherson, and you can work out the details with her."

Dr. McPherson explained to me that the class would meet on November 21, the Tuesday right before Thanksgiving, at a building on the Wake Forest campus called Wingate. She told me to come to room 209 at three o'clock. After the class both she and Maya Angelou would take some time to visit with me. I told her that I looked forward to being there, and I thanked her several times for being such a kind intercessor.

During this momentous phone conversation, the bacon had burned. But the smoky mess in the kitchen wasn't my only problem. I had just agreed to attend a class the Tuesday before Thanksgiving at Wake Forest University in Winston-Salem, North Carolina. I had only a few weeks earlier taken a vow of obedience, which meant that

I couldn't make such a decision on my own. I needed to get permission, retroactively.

I needed to ask Greg, the Jesuit superior, for permission to go to Wake Forest. I didn't have any money for such a venture, so if this was to happen, then I was completely dependent on him and his approval. I couldn't sit on this, because any delay might lessen the possibility of going. I needed to bring this to his attention immediately.

I started to look for him all around the Jesuit community. Sure enough, because it was a Sunday afternoon and the Green Bay Packers were playing, he was in the television room watching the game. They were playing Chicago at Green Bay—this was a big game—and not one that should be interrupted. I entered and sat down to watch with him. When a commercial came on, I turned to him.

"Greg, I have something I really need to talk to you about."

He looked at me and asked what I needed.

I had about ninety seconds, given the commercial cycle, so I decided to cut to the chase. "Well, the American poet Maya Angelou just called me and invited me to attend her class next week at Wake Forest in North Carolina, and then we'd sit for an interview afterward. It's for a paper in Dr. Hook's class. Can I go?"

"Are you serious?"

I quickly gave him some very brief background. I could see he was taking me quite seriously.

"How would you get there?" he asked.

I hadn't thought of that part, yet. I looked at him blankly.

"What about your classes here?"

I hadn't thought of that part either.

"Well this is very interesting, indeed. I need to bring this to the staff to see what they think about it. Can you write up a proposal with possible transportation options and get it to me? If you are allowed to go, you'd need to be back here for Thanksgiving, so keep that in mind as you look at transportation."

I returned to the kitchen to prepare the dinner while also beginning my investigation. I opened the Omaha yellow pages and began to call different car-rental companies—but I learned quickly that since I was under the age of twenty-five, that option wasn't going to work for me. I called Greyhound next and discovered that a Monday departure by bus would get me to Winston-Salem on Wednesday—not very helpful for a Tuesday meeting. I rang Amtrak and learned that the train was already sold out, probably because of a great number of travelers for the upcoming Thanksgiving holiday. Options were beginning to run thin.

After dinner and community prayer, I called several airlines. The flights to Greensboro, North Carolina, were all expensive. Also, Greensboro was thirty miles from Winston-Salem. There was only one airline, US Air, that still had seats available and that would fly directly into the airport in Winston-Salem. But it was pricey.

Besides the results of my research I dug through my own files in order to find a copy of the letter I had sent out after the novitiate pilgrimage to all the people who had been so helpful along the way. I decided to include it with the proposal, along with a duplicate of the recent letter I faxed to Dr. McPherson. I hoped these inclusions would communicate to my superior that there was a somewhat lengthy history to this pursuit. I stuffed all my efforts into a manila envelope and then took this valuable packet and slid it carefully under Greg's bedroom door.

The next morning Greg gave me permission for the trip. It seemed apparent to both of us that God had a plan that was quickly unfolding. Greg wanted me to fly to Winston-Salem so that the trip would be as simple and as safe as possible—a great example of that

Jesuit hallmark of *cura personalis*, the care for the person. He didn't want me to return ragged from excessive travel. Nor did he want me to risk the possibility of missing this important meeting because of a delay or a missed connection. He instructed me to book the ticket immediately—before the end of the day—so that it would qualify for a seven-day advanced purchase.

In anticipation of these travels to North Carolina, I called my old friend Fr. Larry Hunt at Saint Benedict. I asked if he would be willing once again to welcome me during my stay in Winston-Salem. Without a pause he said that it would be a great delight for him—he would love to have the company and I was most welcome.

On Sunday, the day before I was to leave Omaha, I faxed Dr. McPherson simply to confirm our Tuesday class meeting. I left for North Carolina after a full day of classes at Creighton; the flights were problem-free, and I landed on time. When I deplaned in Winston-Salem, I found a smiling old priest outside the gate. Larry Hunt greeted me with a hug and said, "You never know what God can do for us!" Perhaps it was because I was tired from the long day of study and travel, but I found myself tearing up as he embraced me.

We arrived at Saint Benedict, and when Larry showed me to my room, he handed me a note. It was a phone message from Dr. McPherson, who had called earlier. She asked that I telephone her immediately upon my arrival. Larry showed me to the phone, and I placed the call. Dr. McPherson answered with, "Hello, Casey!" Then, "I'm very sorry to have to tell you that we have had to cancel our class for tomorrow."

"What?"

She explained that most of their students were leaving early for Thanksgiving and that with so few remaining, the professors felt it wasn't worth having the class, so they decided to cancel.

I couldn't speak.

But then Dr. McPherson said that she and Maya Angelou had arranged for something better. They decided that I would come to Maya Angelou's house at three thirty the next afternoon for a long afternoon visit and that when we finished our conversation, I would be a guest for dinner at her house. She gave me the address, also the security code for the entrance gate, and said, "I am glad that you are here. I'll look forward to meeting you tomorrow."

I hung up the phone and looked at Larry, who said to me, "In the past two minutes you went from looking like you were going to cry to looking like you just won the lottery." He was right. When I shared with him what had happened, he just smiled.

"You better go to bed," Larry instructed. "You need to be rested, because tomorrow is much more than you know."

He was right again. The next day we had Mass and then, because the morning was free, I decided to visit Elsie Nottingham. Larry shared with me that Clarence had died recently, so I wanted to visit her to pay my respects and to see how she was doing. We had a good visit, and then I returned to Saint Benedict to prepare for the afternoon.

Larry was gracious enough to drop me off at Maya Angelou's house—I suspect mostly because he wanted to find out where exactly she lived! When I arrived, I pressed the intercom button, and then I entered the security code into the keypad at the front entrance gate. The long gate began to roll open, and I was surprised to find that I had arrived at the same time as Dr. McPherson. She greeted me warmly at the front door, and we entered the house together. You can imagine my surprise when we stepped inside and found about twenty people running around! Children were screaming and laughing, and adults were chatting away—it was utter chaos. It was a far different scene from the tranquil image of a poet's house I had imagined.

We stood in the front hall for a moment, and then from right around the corner I heard the voice of Maya Angelou. She stepped into the entrance, and Dr. McPherson introduced us. Upon greeting me, Dr. Angelou turned to a small table and started to pour a glass of wine for me while gesturing for the three of us to sit at a small table near the kitchen for a brief conversation.

While Dr. McPherson and I made our way to the table, Maya Angelou stepped aside to chat with a couple who were standing farther down the hallway. Dr. McPherson explained that just before we arrived, Maya Angelou had returned from the University of Texas, where she had been giving a talk. She was now anticipating the arrival of about a hundred people who would be her Thanksgiving Day guests—the people in the house were the early arrivals.

Soon Maya Angelou joined us, raised her glass for a toast, and said, "Welcome!" We began to visit as early Thanksgiving guests began to leave for their hotels. When the house quieted, she looked at Dr. McPherson and explained that she needed to take a nap because she felt worn from her recent travels. She excused herself and assured us that she would return after her rest and then we could continue our conversation.

This brief interlude turned out to be a good thing because it afforded me time with Dr. McPherson, whom I learned was not merely a good friend of Maya Angelou but also the academic scholar of her autobiography. While studying for her doctorate at the University of Iowa, she wrote her dissertation on Angelou, which was eventually published under the title *Order Out of Chaos: The Autobiographical Works of Maya Angelou*. Our hour-long conversation was incredibly interesting. She explained that people loved Angelou's autobiography because it chronicled growth in personal character, especially through a pattern of "circuitous journey," a way of living that leads ultimately to deeper understanding of human interiority. "You can experience her growth by following the writing. It's a beautiful recording of the human spirit." She also emphasized that people particularly loved the sincere vulnerability contained within both Angelou's poetry and autobiography. "Not many people dare to be honest with their history. They may not be able to do that, but at least they see there are people who are able to do it."

About an hour into our good conversation, Maya Angelou arrived and took her place at the table. She looked at me and said, "You want to talk to me about heroes."

I nodded and stated that I was taking a class at Creighton in ancient literature and that our focus was on attributes of the hero. She paused and reflected for a moment and then said that she wanted to begin by saying something about the humanity of heroes. It was a constant temptation, she said, for human beings to want to believe that there are some among us who are perfect and that the temptation to hold people to a standard of perfection was unjust. "We make the hero flawless. . . . No one is flawless. We are all flawed because we're human."

She told me that it was a pleasure to do this interview with me because I wasn't a member of the media. Her perception was that the media sometimes feeds this temptation by creating illusions of perfection, and then when people make mistakes, the result is scandal and disillusionment. She insisted that we allow the heroes of our culture to be fully human and to recognize that humanity has limitations. "The only way we can have protection from the slings and arrows of the pernicious media is by a steadfast, solid offering of honesty. It's the only way. When the hero says, 'You caught me,'—that's one thing. But when she says, 'I am vulnerable. I am human. I have flaws and faults,' then the viewer, the student, has the opportunity to emulate the hero. . . . In a wonderful way it ties the student into the hero, because without really considering it, the student says, 'That's just like me. I'm very much like that.' The student is at her best when there is an identification with the hero. We become equals. Equals make friends. There is an alliance of equals. Only under these circumstances do real teaching and learning take place."

We continued our conversation but were interrupted by a telephone call, which Maya Angelou took at the table. It was Oprah Winfrey. Although I wasn't *trying* to listen, it was hard not to because Dr. Angelou was sitting right next to me. The call had to do with some concern about Oprah staying at Maya Angelou's other house in Winston-Salem and that her dog was going to be indoors and that there was some issue with Maya's son and that dog.

When the phone conversation ended, I asked, "Why did you agree to meet me after all this time?" I anticipated an answer that would highlight something of my extended efforts—an acknowledgment of my persistence and the distances I had traveled.

Maya Angelou looked at Dolly McPherson and smiled. "Well, now—what a lovely question. Let me see how to answer. Quite often the thinkers of the Catholic Church have been the close readers of the text. They've always been the Jesuits."

I smiled in appreciation.

She leaned in and pushed her chair closer to the table and looked directly into my eyes as she continued. "They have no interaction with African Americans. When they teach our children, they don't know the intellectual community in the black community—no matter how close their reading. I wanted to take the time because you will be a teacher and you need to know that there is in the African American community a way of working, a way of living, that is of the intellect."

McPherson joined in. "You will have influence. And we want to have influence in your future. We're not Catholic—but all roads lead to Rome, so we are united in Jesus, aren't we? For us to speak with a Jesuit who will influence future generations—this is why we agreed. And it is a delight for us to be with you."

I didn't know what to say. What came to my heart in that moment was something from Scripture—from the eighth chapter of the apostle Paul's letter to the Romans: "All things work together for good for those who love God." I felt this deep communion with them as we sat at the table. I realized that I was looking at them with a big grin on my face.

After a moment of sacred silence, I asked Maya Angelou, "What do you think the young struggle with today?"

She paused for a moment. "I don't really see a difference between fifty and five hundred years ago, as far as challenges for young people. The challenge is to live as honestly, honorably, generously, and kindly as possible. That's the challenge. To remain centered as a child of God trying to be kind and generous and patient . . . and blowing it all the time. To be able to wish for and work for kindness, and when you blow it to say sorry."

A moment later she said that there was something unique about the present moment, however, that magnified the difficulty faced by the young. "The temptations seem to be more profound, prevalent, deep, and alluring today."

"Then what gives you hope about us—about the young?" I asked.

Maya Angelou reached across the table and took my hand. She had a firm grip! And when I looked at her she began to smile with the brightest smile my eyes have seen.

"I have a feeling we are in a fabulous time. I seem to sense *an optimism*. It's curious when I look at our world and sense optimism. To see Londonderry, Northern Ireland, the Middle East, Rwanda,

Somalia . . . when I look at our world and see the fighting, the dying. It seems almost childish to see optimism. But something has turned. It's like a pendulum. Sometime it must go back. We are on an upswing. We're on our way up. I can sense it. I believe it. We are on an optimism swing. If you join it, it goes faster. I join it."

"I do, too," I said.

"Good," said Maya Angelou. "That's why you are here, my new Jesuit friend."

It was time for her to help prepare the dinner. She invited me to walk through the house to admire the extensive artwork—all created by African and African American artists and commissioned by her. The most beautiful work I recall seeing was a story quilt of her life, a gift given to her by Oprah Winfrey. As I stood there admiring it, Dr. McPherson walked by and paused. "I had a hunch you'd like that!"

The dinner was extraordinary—not just because of the food but because of the company. Perhaps twenty-five people sat around the large dining room table. To my left was the writer Rosa Guy, who founded what eventually became the Harlem Writers Guild. To my right was Maya Angelou's son, Guy Johnson. Just down from me was Oprah Winfrey. Across the table was Maya Angelou's brother, Bailey. Throughout the meal I kept looking around the table and realizing that I was experiencing something remarkably incarnational. So many people I knew from the written word, but in that moment I knew them no longer merely through text—they were enfleshed before my very eyes, and amazingly, I was in their midst.

After the dinner we went to the basement where William Chapman Nyaho, a pianist from Ghana who taught music in Louisiana, treated us to a little concert. When he finished his recital, Maya Angelou abruptly stood and quickly dismissed us—she was exhausted, and the party was officially over. I remained seated on a couch while she said her good-byes to the guests. I had my backpack with me, and I reached into it to take out some books I wanted her to sign.

When everybody had left, she turned and looked at me sitting there. She said with some annoyance, "Why are you still here?" I told her that I had books I hoped she would sign. She looked frustrated and told me to come back in the morning and that she'd sign them then. I stood up and thanked her for everything, and then she asked, "Where are you staying?" I told her that I was at St. Benedict the Moor.

"How did you get here?"

"I got dropped off."

"How are you getting back?"

I hadn't thought about that. It was late, and I didn't want to call Larry. I stood there and felt embarrassed. She looked at me and rolled her eyes slightly upward. "Wait here."

I think I was pushing my luck. I should have left with the other guests and figured out how to get back to the church on my own. About a minute later she came back into the room and said, "My driver is out front and will take you to St. Benedict. Good night."

I stepped outside and found a limousine waiting. The driver opened the door for me and gestured that I climb inside. When we arrived at St. Benedict, I was concerned that the presence of a limo in front of this simple, tiny church might cause a scene in the neighborhood. I exited quickly and entered the house as quietly as I could, for I didn't want to wake Larry. I went to my room and crawled into bed, my mind overflowing with the memories and graces of the day.

I awoke the next morning to a complete rush as I hurried to prepare for my return to Omaha. I was a sweaty mess on that beautiful North Carolina morning. Somehow I had to get to Maya Angelou's house to pick up those books, and then I needed to get to the airport so that I could make my way back to Omaha. Larry kindly offered to take me to the airport, and he arranged for us to leave a few minutes early so that we could swing by her house. When we got there, I went to the gate and pressed the intercom button. Someone answered and I explained who I was and that I was there to pick up some books I had left for Maya Angelou to sign. The voice on the other end paused. "Is this the Jesuit?"

I said yes, and she gave me the code that opened the gate. I walked up to the door, and someone I hadn't met before had the bag of books ready for me. "Here you go. Happy Thanksgiving!" I took the bag, thanked her, and then returned to the car. Larry drove me to the Winston-Salem airport, and I said goodbye to him for the last time. I watched him drive away, mindful of the many kindnesses that he had shown me in North Carolina.

A while later, I was on the plane and headed home. I reached down into my backpack to retrieve one of the books—the book I had asked her to sign specifically for me—*The Complete Collected Poems of Maya Angelou*. I opened it to the dedication page and read the text already in print: "This book is dedicated to the great love of my life." In lovely handwriting was added my name, Maya Angelou's signature, and the date: November 22, 1995.

When I looked a second time I noticed that she had added one word that was larger than anything else on the page. *Joy!*

These days, at the age of forty-three, as I reflect back upon my life as a Jesuit pilgrim, I feel my heart drawn to a Jesuit companion, one I have not met but whom I have come to love—our good Pope Francis, who apparently has learned much from his own Jesuit pilgrimage as well. I feel a communion with him in these words of his: "Joy adapts and changes, but it always endures, even as a flicker of light born of our personal certainty that, when everything is said and done, we are infinitely loved."[2]

---

2. Pope Francis, *Evangelii Gaudium*, 6.

I am convinced that we who are joyful are so precisely because we know who we are in the eyes of the Father. We are *always* beloved sons and daughters! This knowledge enables each of us to move along with the path, always *adapting to change* in our surroundings because we recognize that nothing human is foreign. We are always in the midst of companionship with other sisters and brothers along the way. Joy, it seems to me, is essentially the knowledge of the heart and mind that no matter what happens in our journey, God is always with us as we move along, revealing himself often through the kindness and gentleness of our fellow sojourners. God remains steadfast in his faithfulness; he would never lead his beloved daughters and sons down a dead end, despite our having moments where, as Thomas Merton described so eloquently, "I may seem to be lost and in the shadow of death." I believe with all my heart, soul, mind, and strength that "*all things work together for good for those who love God*" (italics added). The joy of Maya Angelou seems best expressed by our Pope Francis: "We become fully human when we become more than human, when we let God bring us beyond ourselves in order to attain the fullest truth of our being."[3]

That, my friends, is how the kingfisher catches fire.

---

3. Pope Francis, *Evangelii Gaudium*, 8.

Acknowledgments

I would like to acknowledge the great people I met on pilgrimage. This book serves as a small gesture of gratitude for your kindness.

I'm grateful to the Society of Jesus for the formation its members and benefactors provide and for the great companions I have within the network of Jesuit schools.

I'm grateful to my students who over the years have heard my pilgrimage story and encouraged me to write it down. I'm especially grateful to the students at Boston College who read an early version of the manuscript and provided valuable feedback. I'm thankful for Karen Kiefer, from the Boston College Church in the 21st Century Center, who helped me connect to Loyola Press. At Loyola, Joe Durepos read the manuscript and became an instant source of encouragement. I'm indebted to my editor at Loyola, Vinita Wright, who offered excellent feedback and accompanied me through the process of creating this book. Finally, I express gratitude and affection to my spiritual father and mentor, William Leahy, SJ.

Fr. Casey Beaumier, SJ
Boston College

About the Author

Casey Beaumier, SJ, is director of the Institute for Advanced Jesuit Studies at Boston College, the school from which he received his Ph.D. in United States religious history. He lives in Fenwick Hall, where he serves as mentor and spiritual director for students, seminarians, women religious, and priests.

Continue the Conversation

If you enjoyed this book, then connect with Loyola Press to continue the conversation, engage with other readers, and find out about new and upcoming books from your favorite spiritual writers.

Visit us at **LoyolaPress.com** to create an account and register for our newsletters.

Or scan the code on the left with your smartphone.

Connect with us through:

 **Facebook**
facebook.com
/loyolapress

 **Twitter**
twitter.com
/loyolapress

 **YouTube**
youtube.com
/loyolapress